neon daze

neon daze

amy brown

Victoria University Press

TE WHARE WĀNANGA O TE ŪPOKO O TE IKA A MĀUI

VICTORIA
UNIVERSITY OF WELLINGTON

VICTORIA UNIVERSITY PRESS
Victoria University of Wellington
PO Box 600 Wellington
vup.victoria.ac.nz

A catalogue record is available at the National Library of New Zealand

ISBN 9781776562381

Printed by Ligare, Auckland

for Robin

Contents

1

13 *August 2016*

This day begins early
when seven kilos you'll lose
by its end starts to leak
and your abdomen begins
to speak in a voice that books
and friends recommend you
control as soon as you hear it.[1]

1 To Admit / To Edit

I admit to editing the words written on, near to, or about the declared date. The line breaks above have been arranged and rearranged – into a prose-shaped rectangle, a narrow waist, couplets, quatrains. This entry started life in lines about the length of the hospital serviette on which I wrote the day after giving birth.

'To admit' comes from the Latin *admittere*, meaning to give entrance to or permit, later to let go of or send, and, later still, to concede as being true. 'To edit' also originates from Latin, *editus*, the past participle of *edere*, meaning to give out or publish. An admission, like a confession, lets the hearer in; an edition is a sending forth into the world – a sort of birth. When I began writing this – what I am now calling a verse journal – I did consider how it could be made public (having been conditioned to view publication as a measure of success). But, my right leg was still numb, my breasts were foreign and solid with coming milk, there was a cannula in my left wrist and I couldn't shift my gaze from the eight pounds of my flesh that were lying in the clear plastic bassinet next to my bed. Hands are for holding, not writing; a brain is for counting the hours between feeds, not writing; waking hours are for feeding; sleeping hours are for sleeping. The record of the days did not seem to be mine to share, to give out. I wrote often, privately, for myself, which was at the time an extension of my son – the function of writing being to keep this placenta-like being sane.

Four months passed and I had eighty pages of notes written to myself, most of which I had forgotten writing. Eighty pages can look like a book, especially when you haven't published much in four years. If someone asked if I was managing to write, I said yes. It felt like a lie, because this writing did not count – secret, secreted – and yet there the pages were, ready to be edited. To edit implies an audience. Even imagining myself as reader, I saw the book being hated. In late pregnancy and early motherhood, I have read writer–mothers (Ferrante, Cusk, Paley, Notley, Nelson – all of whom I recommend) describing the conditions of their lives and felt a sense of jealous threat; the more I related to what I read, the more acute the irritation of thinking, Who is she to own this experience that I know just as well? I was protecting my making meaning from a universal, domestic circumstance, as common and taboo as bodily fluids. Perhaps it was the same character flaw that caused me to peel away from the mothers' group – this insecure act of comparison. My baby is slow to roll over; my writing dwells too

Understand the sound
is temporary, discern its meaning
and reply in your own strong
timbre – numbers, colours, stamps
of feet. Olympic sprinters cease
to distract, so find the ground
through the roar, forehead
pressing an orange Swiss ball,
rolling right to left, and try to let
the rubber's squeal against the floor,
sanitiser, grooves and ridges smother
what they say lasts forty seconds
but all they see is you – deafened –
and green figures on the screen,
line spiking across a long tongue
made of childhood printer paper –
perforated edges good for tearing.

When you're told the voice has no meaning
its volume soars and you shudder with bass.
The monstrous tenor is for an anaesthetist
whose task is to insert a line while you writhe.
crucial to stay still now   and somehow you do.
The scream extinguishes itself like a burning
cold; in this way you are petrified, legs dangle
off the bed's high side, back bare marble,

much on sleep; my experience of birth was of deafening volume whereas Maggie Nelson called
it the quietest time of her life.

A writer acquaintance warned, in an interview, against comparison. As I read this
interview I recalled a conversation between us at my last book launch; she'd commented, with
a tone of encouragement, on the width of the epic's spine – its heft. It's nothing compared with
yours, I'd said, referring to her recently published eight-hundred-page novel. Her expression
flickered. Yes, I thought, ashamed, it was ungracious not to take the compliment. Wrong to
compare. Of course, we each send different things out into the world, have incomparable sins
to admit to and audiences to admit.

head tucked to hide what your face hears.
In the divine quiet you raise a smile, see people
in the room, even talk to them on human terms.
You are worryingly calm, the obstetrician says
after an hour of trying to imagine the diaphragm
as a stainless-steel coffee plunger (a book's idea;
not your own). Can you still feel it? a midwife asks,
curious. Yep. But it does not belong to you, or
you do not belong to you (the first taste). A wringing
wave, of course you can feel it. And the doctor wiping
away what must be faeces. Are you an athlete?
Conversational between pushes.[2] No. Too late
to run when numb from the ribs down.

Next come implements: a Ventouse cup, forceps
before an emergency caesarean. A bit Shakespearean,
preparing for act three, carried like a soap-opera patient
by five hospital staff from bed to bed. Don't try to help,
warns a new anaesthetist, oblivious to the oddness
of your day – what is to her a Saturday nightshift.
Her absence of empathy tranquillises. You attempt to
impress with small jokes while waiting to enter the theatre –
are you audience or star? She rubs ice over your calf, stomach

2 To Push
You are a good pusher, the obstetrician said the next day. I'm sure there will be no trouble next time. There was trouble this time. I wondered as he examined my episiotomy and congratulated us both on the healing wound whether it is best practice – a policy suggested at a conference, perhaps – to convince the new mother whose baby gets stuck that she is in fact capable of propelling the creature out of herself using her own muscles – that it is not her fault that she, two midwives, two obstetricians (one for each end, should the foetus need to be pushed back in and tugged out through a caesarean section), an anaesthetist and a neonatologist (to check the distressed infant) ended up in theatre for two hours on a Saturday evening. 'Push' is a relic of a word, its root fittingly violent – from *pel*, meaning to thrust, strike and drive. Pell-mell, I think. But that is a different 'pell' – the pell that comes from 'skin' in French (*peau*) and 'mell' from *mêlée*, to mix. A confusion of skins.

13

and cheek, charting the limits of feeling across the shocked
regions. The obstetrician squeezes your trembling hand,
kind rather than clinical. Normal – due to the epidural.
Violent tremors for an hour, covered in blankets warm
from a bed-linen oven. And then, at last, under the stage lights
you're halved like any leggy assistant about to be sawn,
an off-white blanket clipped to two metal bars, hiding waist
down from top up. The magician wears a plastic shield over
his glasses – you know why. Later, as he peers over the partition
the visor is brightly freckled, but by then you have the blue-eyed
fish of a son on your chest and cannot hear *haemorrhage*, only
the neonate being deemed nice and pink with a good squawk.

You watch your husband as he fits the hand-knitted hat
over the crop circle laceration left by the Ventouse cup.
You watch, intent; the magician's boxes spin – legs and
torso divide. For now, there is no need to know what is
being sewn; competent urgency; deep puddle on cream
lino like a plait dropped under the chair at the hairdresser's.
Your concern is for the site where the new life lies –
the end that touches and feels. Old imperatives of walking,
showering, and emptying bowels are anaemic and weak.
Soon the epidural will wear off and your lower half will
return to normal, you – naïve – believe.

14 August 2016

The day begins
early, fast broken
with paracetamol
ibuprofen, oxycodone,
a jug of iced water
too heavy to lift.

I want the toast and tea
a friend was given, but
it doesn't come, so resort
to Apricot Delights
intended to sustain me
during yesterday's labour.
Naked with a wad of something
wet between my legs, a token
gown draped across my stomach
and our son on my chest,
I admire him foraging
for sustenance and share
his brilliant hunger.
Kicking strong frog legs,
snuffling, maw wide and blunt,
nose swiping from side
to side, he senses the right
place to anchor himself and drives
forward with all the power
a minutes-old neck can possess,
as if the nipple and aureole were prey
about to escape, he catches his first
meal; the trap of his mouth closes,
sucks and we are both sated.[3]

3 To Sate
I was satisfied, both emptied and filled (a paradox which has become familiar during the last seventeen months). The Old English root, *sadian*, has the exact double meaning of being sated and becoming weary. When the baby feeds he sleeps. The states are synchronous. If one is compromised so is the other. Even now, when feeding (failing to wean . . .), as the milk is let down and the prolactin flows, I can't keep my eyelids open. My pulse slows. As soon as his toddler teeth graze the nipple and he pulls away to ask for a story or to lie on his stomach and push himself off the sofa, his feet finding the floor and taking him to the irresistible, forbidden lamp, as soon as he stops drinking, I wake from my chemical weariness. He is full and satisfied, the lamp's cord between his fat little fingers. I switch back on.

15 August 2016

This was his due date. Now it is his second full day in the world
that is the Mercy, a land of bread and jam for breakfast, chicken
soup for lunch and shepherd's pie for dinner; pastel meals and
constant observation: blood pressure, temperature, head wound;
painkillers (pairs of precise midwives doling out the opiates)
and feeds – a word that I used to associate with chaff, molasses,
enormous nostrils in dirty buckets, but which now means milk.
The days are measured in trays of food and cries of hunger. When
we're moved to a single room, the view over Heidelberg
to the Dandenong Ranges gives us more layers. We are awake when
the sun starts running into the night and the sky turns the colour of brake
lights on Burgundy Street. We are awake when the school bell rings and
children seep out of classrooms onto the AstroTurf playground.
That you will be such a child is more than I can consider. My throat
won't untie. The knots are tightened by a sudden lack of oestrogen
since the placenta left, but it is dishonest to say it is just hormones
making the salt and sugar spill over. I lay him against my thighs and,
eye to eye, we both recognise something awful – that I am his best
chance. It is the twenty-year-old midwife saying I have let my baby
get too cold and need a lesson in tight swaddling. It is touching
hair, beard, body and finding nothing but a coarse version of our son.
Too wiry and weighty. Absolute amnesia of how to love adult shapes.

16 August 2016

A good day is one in which I've not done too much
wrong by you. I say I dislike condescension,
but really it is censure. A good day is one in which you
have your first bath. As instructed, my wrist cushions
the back of your neck. My hand holds your left armpit
and the rest of you is allowed simply to float on the warm

water. Does this warm water resemble your first
warm water?[4] This is your first flannel, your first towel,
our first view of your face wiped clean of all struggle,
stunned by your unswaddled buoyancy.

17 August 2016

Today begins early and is different.
It involves lacing shoes,
packing our suitcase, strapping
you into a black capsule (as if
you were another painkiller
to be swallowed),
and leaving with a box of roses,
lilies and stock, wrongly expecting
a farewell party crowded with everyone
here I've liked. The hospital is not Oz.
We sink into the basement car park
still wearing in-patient bracelets.

Perhaps he sees my breathing,
holding in the largest part of what

---

4 To Repeat
Écoutez répétez, my seventh-form French teacher would chant. Each time we'd listen and
repeat, the words would change – why would the task be set if our pronunciation did not
improve? When anyone claims that the definition of insanity is doing something repeatedly
and expecting a different result, I wonder whether it is in fact possible to do the same thing
twice, when the conditions in which you are acting keep changing. There are many variables
with babies; their requirements are simple but the subtle ways in which the requirements can
be finessed and refined can drive you insane. I think I write about this in a later entry, but it
is worth repeating.

In this entry the repetition of 'warm water' troubled me. I took it out and rewrote it over
and over, dissatisfied with anything but the exhausted sense of having run out of other, hotter
or colder words. It disappoints me that 'luke' alone cannot be a temperature.

I feel and letting out in small sighs
the fright of being free. So easy
to leave with a whole new person.
He strides about the car park
as if he's lost the car, swinging
the black capsule of you,
saying, silly-voiced, This is a lesson
in how to avoid being followed.
My sense of humour is smothered.
We must click the capsule into the base
in the backseat and amidst the thick
scents of flowers and your mother,
whose finger you hold to comfort her,
you, baby, will be taken home.

On the drive,
I want to point out landmarks, but
my voice is ornamental – too fragile
for use and I've forgotten where we are.

18 August 2016

We achieve small tasks between caring for our son. You separate the
boxed flowers into all the suitable vessels – gladioli and gerberas in
a rusty enamel pitcher; roses in a Rose's Breakfast Marmalade jar. I
call Centrelink and try to communicate. What is your child's name?
I spell it out before understanding she is only asking out of interest.
Congratulations, she says. In the afternoon, I walk with stiff steps
around the block, my right leg still weird, but carrying less weight. I
think people look at me as if I have escaped, and feel that perhaps I
have. At the corner store I buy us Rocky Roads. There is a mirror above
the counter, angled to catch thieves.

19 August 2016

Lions, elephants and bees
hang over the stair rail,
their wetness fogging
the windows.

Outside, the cyclamen
gives up – its flowers and
leaves are floppy as a six-
day-old under the weight

of raindrops. It is a humid life –
leaks of milk, blood, tears,
changing soaked bed linen,
filling a small teal tub with

warm[5] water and squeezing
a flannel over the dried blood
still matted in hair. The churn
of the washing machine, the hum

of rain, the wheezing baby's mouth
bubbling with milk, the unnerving
pulse of lochia as he sucks.

---

5 To Define
My thesaurus says 'deep' is a synonym for 'warm'. The water would have been fifteen centimetres
deep at most. Its temperature like blood. Its meaning as deep as the cot's, the couch's, the
swaddle's, the pram's – anything that holds or carries his body gains significance.

This Christmas he received a book called *General Relativity for Babies*, which defines a
black hole as a large amount of mass in a relatively small area. You are our little black hole, I
tell him. The more I think about it, the more apt the analogy seems. *A black hole has so much
mass that not even light can escape its warp* . . .

20 August 2016

Alive almost exactly
one week. The most
important thing is to
sleep. When you sleep
you sound like you're dying.
Under my eyelids you are
drowning in milk – lungfuls
of white and cream. But
when the retinas have had
an hour's dreaming rest
the effect is like a saline bath,
rinsing away the sting and
burn of being awake, you lie
perfect on a white towel,
head to one side – the sort
of profile that should be
pressed on a coin – and
your chest's rise is only
just perceptible; the yellowish
skin where your throat and
collar meet, filling with and
emptying air. You are almost
exactly one week old and
you are asleep.

21 August 2016

Our days are diced
into baby-sized
pieces; chew slowly
so as not to choke.

Taste the twelve
mornings in each
twenty-four hours
and try to enjoy
twelve bedtimes too.
(And twelve breakfasts,
why not?) A day is
measured by suckling
for twenty to fifty minutes,
one or two nappies filled,
one or two fresh suits.
And sometimes he is bathed
in a blinding version of
his first weightless state.

22 August 2016

Treat it as you would a sprained ankle
the Canadian physio advises – rest, ice,
compression, elevation. A little exercise
is beneficial – blood flow aids healing, but
never continue through the pain. Pain
ranges from one to ten. Until a week ago
I thought this scale ridiculous. Not knowing
what ten felt like, it made no sense.
I use the pram as a walking frame,
holding my weight in my arms rather
than my legs. The sutures in the middle
of me are different from but neither better
nor worse than expected.[6] The ache grips

6 To Expect
I was surprised, a friend said on New Year's Eve, when you said you hadn't expected having
a baby to be hard. I paraphrase poorly, quote out of context, emphasise the aspects of the
sentiment that stung. This friend didn't mean any harm. I tried to explain that all imaginings
were thin and theoretical in comparison with the actual. You could listen to new mothers

the buttocks and upper thigh, the walls
he was pushed against. In the shower
my hand doesn't mean to brush what feels
like meaty cross-stitch. I don't want to look,
using a mirror and confronting fear
as the physio suggests. You will soon
have your body back, a colleague says,
then corrects herself: Some parts – others
will go. Others will take months or years
to be yours again. Maybe they will never
belong, because the whole of you is changing.
Even the posture of your silhouette is strange.

23 August 2016

During the night feeds, I listen to a podcast
about Virginia Woolf and hear only
fragments of it – the stones in her pockets;
that if she were alive today she would be
a comedian. I listen with one earbud in,
the other ear devoted to your repertoire
of grunts and squeals. I stare at us reflected
in the wardrobe mirror, admiring the scene's
composition and wishing I could photograph it,
but the phone would ruin the image. And,
you would not tolerate my hand leaving you
for such fripperies. Some time in between

say they were sleeping for forty-five minutes at a time and feeding every two hours. This
information could be known and, to an extent, braced for. 'Expect' comes from the Latin,
exspectare, meaning 'to look out for'. 'To look' is the shadow of 'to feel'. Later I mention Dante's
bright heaven as an analogy for the bright newness of this experience, but what I actually have
in mind is the condition of Plato's prisoner, at last released from the cave and seeing the sources
of the shadows on the wall – the donkey's feathered fetlocks in all their greyish yellow glory.

dozing and feeding, hoisting your three and
a half kilos from breast to shoulder – rubbing
the back – I confuse you with the subject of
the podcast. Or with me. One of us is like
Virginia and knowing this causes the tears
again. It has only been ten days and already
I am hallucinating.[7] You are not yet the age
for 'purple' crying. The word *inconsolable* is hard
as a stone in the pocket of the night. But,
as the windows pale, and the chance of a hot
shower approaches, its meaning weighs less.
Even your body lightens with the dawn.

24 August 2016

Opening the blinds and mopping
condensation from the window
is like sluicing one's face or
taking vitamin D tablets. Sun
bleaches the table. Opposite the tall
window, our neighbour in his early
twenties rolls up his own blind.
We are five metres apart, upstairs,

7 To Hallucinate
No, I didn't literally believe Virginia Woolf was in the nursery. The almost pleasurable
disturbance (what would no doubt have been defined as hysteria by a medical professional in
recent history – perhaps even by my doctor husband, had I woken him and tried to explain
the source of my upset; and, indeed, the psychological turmoil could be said to stem from the
womb on this occasion) came from the fatigue-induced sense that all I saw and heard and
felt seemed equally illusive. The Attic origin of 'hallucinate' is *halyein*, meaning to wander in
mind, or be at a loss, or be beside oneself (with joy or sorrow). That is what I was doing, with
myself in my arms, my reflection divided, a literal voice in my ear and the ghost of a feminist
predecessor filling what is the opposite of a room of one's own. A nursery is a place in which
you belong to someone else.

gaping across the bright courtyard
into each other's morning. He is
wearing boxer shorts and yawning.
I am holding you and have my shirt
unbuttoned, half of the feeding bra
open, one Amazonian breast showing.

25 August 2016

The baby is turning into a cat or a pig
or a lamb and I am turning into a baby,
lying where the infant was placed an hour
ago while the swaddle was arranged.
I wake from naps unsure of where I am,
who I am, only certain of the creature
in the bassinet growling or mewling or
bleating. I am secreting almost as much
as the baby. As I feed him, I drink litres
of milk. People provide me with meals and
my job is to sleep when he sleeps. Eat
before he drinks. Keep ourselves clean and
dry. He grimaces and goes puce while
I hold sutures and lean forward, stomach
over thighs, tiptoeing in lieu of using
the footstool prescribed by the physio.

26 August 2016

Sleep fits tightly inside
thirty minutes. Its shape
corseted and unfamiliar,
especially the tail end

in which I hear him
somewhere nearby –
nearer than he ever is –
under me or back inside.
I never remember
placing him in his cot
inside his own half hour
of condensed solitude.

Sketch

a shining milky sneer, ragdoll neck
doubling chins, jagged fingernails
urgent lungs, saluting fists, glazed
cobalt eyes, blistered Cupid's bow
dried blood in his ears, hair growing
in whorls, warm weight on the palm

27 August 2016

I have no kitchen duties.
I lie on the couch and like
a young god he drinks
from me, both of us serene,
while everyone else prepares
marinated chicken and baked
quinces. Would you like to smell?
his aunt asks and I nod, accepting
all such offerings as a goddess
ought. Yes, the whole fruit
with its waxy yellow skin does
remind me of pineapple; yes,

the naked quarter smells acidic,
like the wine I won't drink.

28 August 2016

Things I have considered today other than my son:
the Russian zookeeper's lace-fronted dress and the way
her pet cat let the squirrel monkey grip its fur and ride
on its back (but honestly this reminded me of the baby);
and Georgia O'Keeffe's paintings posted by a travelling
poet friend to social media. I wondered whether the shapes
were really feminine (eggy, breasty, rounded edges)
the colours pastel Rothkos or if I was merely projecting.

29 August 2016

Instead of sleeping
I push you to Dights Falls.

As well as sleeping
you smell mown grass

and wattle pollen.
Instead of sleeping I admire

dogs – pairs of fox terriers,
lone collies, something

intelligent-looking with one
milk blue eye. While sleeping

you hold the pram belt
to your mouth and nose.

Instead of sleeping
I watch you dream.[8]

31 August 2016

The story of the red shoes
scared me – not a dancer[9]
at the best of times,
claustrophobic in clothes
too tight to be removed.
But now, with you, little
bomb, strapped to my body
with my own arms, threatening
to explode if I stop swaying
and prancing to Egyptian
jazz, I am close to living
the fairy tale. The nurse
asks if I am familiar with
Pavlov's Dog. I say yes, but
she tells the story anyway.

8 To Dream
He has been dreaming since he was a foetus, I am led to believe by internet forums that discuss such questions. Illusions, phantasms, deceptions existent even or especially in utero.

9 To Dance
Now, at nearly a year and a half, he dances without me, better than me, uninhibited, instinctive. Within seconds he knows whether he likes or dislikes a song. If we are in the car and he yells, I know to change the station. His taste is good, I think. Motown is popular. The dancing entails arm flailing – a decisive shaking from elbow to fingertips. If he is holding a maraca, all the better. Out of the car seat, the legs might join in, bending at the knees in a shallow, rhythmic squat. If I do a silly pirouette it is met with the sort of joy that throws him onto his mat in a parodic stunt of the spin gone wrong.

A shush might be enough,
if associated with his cot.
Yet here I am lurching
like the bus in *Speed* and
whistling a breathy prayer
that you will sleep. And then
what? Will I sleep too?
There is always wet washing,
full rubbish bags, unwritten
words. I'd like to keep living
in this suburb (nothing else
must change now) and consider
ways of raising money to buy
a house. As usual, my only
answer is to write. This time
I believe in the plan – see a link
between two thousand words a day
and wealth. A post-partum mirage.

Pacing Poem

Past the green flowers
past the red stool
past the drying towels
past the letter from school
past the newspapers
past the glass fruit bowl
past the decanter
past the 'Hoptimist' doll
and into the kitchen.

Past the oven
past the breadbin
past the broken dishwasher
past the empty tomato tin
and towards the table.

Around the red chair
over the floorboards
past the stairs
and onto the rug.

Past the lamp
past the outside world
past the radio
past the Argentinian print
and around the bassinet.

Past the novels
past the poetry
past the proteas
past the pottery
and into the sun.

Past the breeze
past the ottoman
past the unwrapped cheese
past the pestle
past the wine rack

nestled
under my armpit:

                                        two deep eyes
                                    still shining wide,

                                    so we keep circling
                                    until sleep arrives.[10]

1 September 2016

Mine is the child that stands
on the adult's feet in order
to learn the steps. Yours leads.
When you falter or trip
I fall too – fall out of sleep and
back into the bewildering
world. It is spring but
the glass is dense with rain.
While I feed you, a timer goes off
telling me the banana bread is
ready. I hold you awkwardly
against my breast, not wanting

10 To Rhyme

It is a fundamental music. I read and his fist starts pumping the air as if a drum solo is playing on the radio. It is incantation – at the witching hour I recite Margaret Wise Brown's *Goodnight Moon*; every bedtime before he is put in his cot, we take a turn around the great green room with the 'telephone, and red balloon and a picture of the cow jumping over the moon'. Brown never had a child, nor liked them much, and possessed no special desire to write children's books, despite having made what I think is a perfect example. She wanted to be a serious modernist – a Gertrude Stein or Virginia Woolf. She believed she was stuck in childhood. 'The first great wonder at the world is big in me, that is the real reason I write.' And she never grew to be old. At forty-two, after an appendectomy, she proved to a nurse she was well again by throwing her leg up in a can-can kick. This sent a blood clot to her brain, which killed her later that day. (I tell Nick this story and he says it's impossible, unless Brown had a hole in her heart. More likely, she would have died of a pulmonary embolism. The can-can kick wouldn't have dislodged the clot. 'Fanciful,' he says, as if fancy is something to eschew.)

you to assume I am putting
you in the oven, and retrieve
the baking. It has a golden
brown peak and thick crust
delicious from being forgotten.

2 September 2016

The world is curling at the edges.
The stork on the greeting
card seems to be flying straight
off the paper with his snug
bundle. On our walk in the park
it is impossible not to notice the flowers
are all the same shade of yellow –
at least five or six different species.
It is the sort of detail
I tell you about. My hands
are affected too, so used
over the last three weeks
to the texture of new skin,
to carrying only four kilos, when
I touch your[11] father's arm it still

11 To Address
A dutiful or courteous approach was this verb's original meaning. To whom should I address
these entries? My sense of duty is primarily to my son – the extraordinary mass of meaning
within a tiny area, container of all light and love that used to radiate over other parts of my life,
including my son's father, my husband, my partner, Nick, him, you. Common truth (a parental
version of the seven-year itch) states that it is three years before the sense of duty and courtesy
to the other parent of your child returns. When it seems we have no ability or inclination to
show kindness to the other, we lavish our love upon the person who contains parts of us both
and in this way we are courteous, our duty is met, the love is sheltered in a new address, a
disturbed version of our old space-time. He is someone's child, too, I think when 'despise'
is the word at the front of mind – when there is anger pressing tight as swimming goggles

feels especially solid and wiry. I'm
unaccustomed to an adult body, I say
when he hugs me. What I mean is
I miss wanting it. Instead of holding
each other directly, we do so via
you – both of us and neither.
As you gain your seventy-five
grams per day, it is easier
to remember that your baby
self is temporary; your one body
will give us many sons.
Your father once told me that
we love our friends best until
we have a partner, then we love
our partner best until we have a
child, and then we love our child
best of all – that, he said, is the way
the world works. I didn't believe
at the time that I would love his
baby better than I loved him.

3 September 2016

Friends bring cinnamon buns and
a fragile native orchid. They hold the baby
and provide adult conversation.
Through hangovers, they are sharper and
quicker than I am. I see their pity
as I try to contribute an analogy involving

around my eyes. I wouldn't want anyone to feel this way about Robin. One day, someone
probably will and I won't be there to help or defend or explain. The only hope is to be as kind
to everyone as I intend to be to my baby.

first ladies' gowns as diplomatic tools.
They understand, you say, after they've left
and I complain of feeling dull (which is really
just in comparison with the neon glare life
has adopted). What do they understand?
That new mothers can be swaddled too
in their own tangles of muslin – squinting out
at the unfamiliar living room with a bloodshot
version of their baby's stare. Baby blue
should be the greyish navy of open water,
not the faded wash of a burning sky –
that is the sublime shade of neonatal irises.

4 September 2016

Downstairs, your father is ironing shirts;
upstairs I am sort of writing. You are grizzling.
We are listening to Sir Michael Marmot's
Boyer Lecture on the social determinants
of health. Lying in a white bassinet below
a shelf of books belonging to parents who
together completed about forty-five years
of education, you are less likely to suffer
from diabetes, heart disease, renal failure
than your thousand counterparts born on
the same day to parents who did not finish
high school. Helpless silkworm
with your fat cheeks and white muslin tail,
unvaccinated, still in the neonatal
danger zone, you are luckier than some,
less lucky than others.

5 September 2016

A mystery is the least fitting thing
to read. A friend prescribes short stories
instead, so I open Janet Frame's
You are now entering the human heart,
a collection of close-ups taken
at an angle as far above plot
as where we currently float.
A child–adult voice shows exactly how
an emotion attaches itself to an almost
random object, like language, like names,
like similes. The stories are short and sit
snug between half-hour naps and half-hour
feeds. They are as comforting as a deep
cup of tea. Why are you crying? he asks
when we brush our teeth. I tell him I am
tired. He says, You are allowed to be tired,
but that is no reason to be upset. I say,
You don't understand how this works.
He says, Yes, but I don't know what
you expect me to do. I say, Nothing.

6 September 2016

He is thinking of next winter,[12] when
the boy will be nearly a whole year
old and it will be three years since

12 To Winter
We passed the winter in question in our rented townhouse in Northcote. I marked piles of essays on *Medea*, he finished the pilot study for his PhD, you strengthened your immune system with a steady succession of febrile viruses shared by your daycare peers.

our last holiday. He is picturing a
pool whose water blends into the view
of the sea. He wants at least twenty-seven
degrees and a balcony. Would you stay
at somewhere called 'Pinnacles'?
Look at that vista. Look at that suite.
He wants me to browse websites, but
the baby has just fallen asleep and it is
eleven o'clock and we are in bed. Paradise
Cove does not compare with an extinguished
lamp and pillowcase against my face for one
or two hopeful hours before trying to reunite
feet with slippers and let my arms find their way
into dressing-gown sleeves as our son howls.

During the day, while he's at work,
I waste time browsing Queensland resorts,
South Pacific retreats, eco lodges and five-
night deals. White sand feels like cheating, too
obviously appealing. I critique loungers lined up
as if ready to drink from kidney-shaped pools.
Is it a frugal relic of a Presbyterian upbringing,
or a hangover influence of my punk ex-boyfriend,
or something else that makes me distrust resorts?
What would my ex-PhD supervisor think;
where would he stay? I wonder at this question
that appears, sudden and involuntary.
The options that involve animals, fruit, walks –
whale-watching, cassowaries, tropical orchards –
are passable. I can pretend that the trip is
beneficial rather than hedonistic – educative.
Dishonest in the same way that I am now pretending
to write, but really hiding from the other Word
document, the unfinished novel.

7 September 2016

'Birthday' has new connotations.
Today is my mother's.[13] I imagine
the state of obstetric care in New Zealand
sixty-seven years ago. I think of my mother
and her own 'geriatric' pregnancy
thirty-two years ago. The labour lasted
ten hours, finished at lunchtime, and
I was a heavy baby. That is the myth.
Never before have I associated the cake
and books and lined forehead with pain,
blood, with a rolling tug that still twists
in my middle nearly four weeks after
the event. I can see the fruit of labour
in a hazy outline through the white mesh
wall of his bassinet and hear breathy
spluttering. He's bigger, bigger
than he was this morning, his father says,
holding him in the evening after a long
day at work. Already growing and ageing,
expanding towards his first birthday,

---

13 To Resolve
At our Gatsbyish friend's New Year's Eve party, he, who admits to relishing organised fun, made each of his forty guests write a resolution and put it into a hat. When nearly all were seated, he silenced the room and made each guest take a resolution from the hat. *My name is ___ and I will ___* was the stipulated formula. When I pulled mine out of the hat my nerves at speaking in front of a room of people were softened by several glasses of wine (my first night away from our child). My name is Amy and I will treat my mother like a human being. Before dinner, while swimming in the silty dam, whose patches of warm and cold are inexplicably distinct, we asked a psychiatrist friend why it is that we so dislike the people we become when around our mothers. I've been trying to block out Christmas – thanks for bringing it all back, was all he said. As a mother now, I find this a bit disturbing, I said. No one replied. Any statement that starts with 'as a mother' tends to sound obnoxious (another manifestation of mother-dismissal).

away from the day of emergence. The red
forceps mark has faded completely;
the scabbed yarmulke left by the Ventouse
has gone too. The crooked nose
straightened and the face has fattened
to the extent that the cheeks quiver
when his pram is pushed over gravel.

8 September 2016

Today the boy sang. I was going to write *sang to me* but that's a false presumption. He didn't even sing to himself but seemed to be letting his voice stretch and kick as his legs do under the swaddle. A faint cooing, like a shy attempt at a dove's call, a pure sound – less spluttering or guttural than his usual milky noises – which I cannot return, and when I try the effect is as unsatisfactory as my whistling. In his sleep, with his pink gums bared, he made a note as reedy and surprising as the couple of occasions when my clarinet produced the sound I meant it to, and it seemed to summon or serenade someone like the Pan in *Wind in the Willows* who saves the baby otter, Portly. Ratty and Mole, who witness this, have their memories of the salvation erased, perhaps to make the drabness of everyday life to which they must return tolerable – to avoid celestially unfair comparisons. I hope Pan came at my son's sleeping call, and I hope my son remembers the song.

9 September 2016

In the last three days I haven't gone past the front steps.
The edge of the balcony is my limit.
A trip to the recycling bin stretches what he's deemed regulation.
I am becoming yin to the sofa's yang as my injury heals.[14]
While we re-watch Nigella cubing Gruyère for a fondue, whipping cream
and describing the significance of eggs en cocotte, you suck my nose
and kick my stomach, demanding more.

10 September 2016

The back of the notebook is catching up
to the front – three crooked columns
and rows and rows of data recording
when the baby feeds and fills a nappy
and special events like baths.
Only four pages now between caring
for the infant and lines of words that
make me feel more myself. I'm angry
at the baby's father, who is downstairs –
doing nothing blameworthy,
cleaning, in fact. I'm angry because
he suggested throwing away an ugly
ceramic owl given to me by my students
this year that is taking up space in

---

14   To Heal
In *The Lost Child*, Ferrante writes, 'Your heart shatters: you can't bear staying together with yourself and you have certain thoughts you can't say.' In *The Argonauts*, Nelson describes the same sensation as a perpetual falling apart, but implies that this need not be painful. Sixteen months on, the pain is gone. New Year's Eve, in a tent ticking with grasshoppers, and swaying with breeze and pleasure, together we test the site where the edges have been fused and the hurt is at first tender, then silent.

the bathroom cupboard required for excess
toilet paper and cakes of soap on which he's
stocked up at Costco. I tell him it's only
a small thing, an unusual possession of my own.
I think of the other parts of myself I've disposed of
or hidden or had cut to size in order to fit
our life together. I'm angry with myself.

11 September 2016

It is the fifteenth anniversary of a terrorist attack.
Today my world is four and a half kilos,
roughly fifty-five centimetres in length.
Wordless, noisy, repetitive.

From my new position in the corner of the rug
I stare into the world's oceans and then
turn my head to try to see what he sees.
My myopic god likes light and movement.

I'm still the same person in this new world –
a procrastinator and corner-cutter and pretender –
but I find odd muscles hurting in my neck and back
and shoulder. It's not the weight of the world

but its omnipresence. Carrying a strange burden
while attempting to continue old tasks requires
certain contortions. While the world is sleeping,
I leap into action. Sleep too, or hang wet towels

or wash dishes or eat lunch or write a poem or
open the Word document in which something
wilts like the unwatered orchid, or water
the orchid or photograph the world at rest.

12 September 2016

It is not unusual for someone in this situation to cry frequently,
at apparently little provocation. I try to stop at slicked eyes and a
swallowing throat – no actual sobs or racing tears – when watching
almost any news story or listening to any song with a cello or piano,
or imagining any scenario in which the child is in harm's way. Aleppo,
the Royal Commission into Institutional Responses to Child Abuse,
the disappearance of a toddler two years ago. It's not empathy, but a
compulsion to see the baby in every situation.

2

13 September 2016

The questionnaire wants to know how often I feel sad or
miserable, whether I blame myself unnecessarily, and if I am
overwhelmed. There are five options to be underlined –
no, never; *hardly ever*; *yes, sometimes*; *fairly often*; *frequently*.
Each answer correlates with a number. *No* may be zero or
five depending on the question. If my numbers total twelve
or more, I will be referred to a GP for psychiatric care.
Mostly honest, I score seven, and then try to whittle
the total down to five. I notice how stigmatised the subject
is in my own desire to minimise symptoms and in the nurse's
assurance that the problems are often physical – thyroid-
related or to do with too little sleep or food. I am comforted.

14 September 2016

It's a good sign that he squints when the blinds
go up. This is a ritual to help us distinguish
between night and day, even if the weather
is wet and grey. I told him in the middle
of the small hours that we were lucky
to be hearing such a lot of water pelting the roof
and to feel warm, dry and quiet. How many others
heard the rain? The nurse's suggestion: Remember
all the mothers around the city, awake, feeding
their babies at the same time as you, to make
the dark less lonely. But I'm an only child –
accustomed to solo ventures, apparently less
fond of sharing. That we seemed to own
the heavy shower was a comfort.
While others download rain on a tin roof,
we listen to a private live performance.

It makes trying to sleep
on the couch under the pilled antimacassar
while the baby lies in his bassinet, choking and
hissing like a tomcat trapped inside the box
of sleep more tolerable: a deliberate
camp-out rather than a retreat from the real
bedroom where the person who goes out
into the day each morning – whose life is still
dilated wide – rests undisturbed by the baby's
guttural calls, my shushing, and the rain.

15 September 2016

Why has this couple visited us? They bring
strawberries, soft cheeses, water crackers and
marinated olives. I put you in the arms of
the man and notice you flinch at the cold
leather jacket sleeve. When I ask how they are,
the woman says, Up and down, as you well know.
I don't know anything; not well, at least.
The woman in her sheer coral-coloured shirt
understands how to comfort a newborn.
When she takes my son from her husband,
she sways and paces and pats as I have just learnt
to do. You have to keep a baby moving,
she tells her husband, otherwise they realise
they're alive and become afraid of dying.

16 September 2016

I mind the repetition less if there isn't someone else
present who might relieve me from it. The rhythm

of my palm beating the baby's back seems crass
and dull compared with the clicks of his
fingertips on his keyboard. I am trying to soothe
and silence the hiccups and yowls; he is writing
assessments of scientific abstracts. He is working.
I am caring for our son and trying to type
one-handed, the few thoughts that need to be
expelled each day as the air in the baby needs
to be removed with constant pats.

17 September 2016

Saturdays are supposed to be days of rest.
I still forget that I don't need to set an alarm.
You, reliable child, go off, I get up, the dressing gown
is always inside out and upside down, slippers
wrong-footed, air cold, your voice gathering volume,
phone, notebook and pen never quite fit properly
in my pocket. Saturdays are for relatively unrushed
showers, while your father supervises you and tries
to cook chipolatas and eggs. He describes you
as a full-time undertaking. I eat my sausages
one-handed while rocking the bassinet as if it were
a boat, gliding you backwards and forward in the stream
of morning sunshine and imagining letting go, letting
you float like Moses across the floorboards.

18 September 2016

More visitors. What happens during your day?
one of the men asks. I tell him it is divided
into two- or three-hour portions: feed, settle,

sleep, repeat. But, says the other, whom I used
to share an office with when we were both
PhD students rather than one successful academic
and one new mother slash unemployed high school
teacher. But, he says, you have time to read?
Several years back, I asked another new parent
the same question and received a cold reply.
Don't ask that! Her brain is addled with sleep
deprivation, scolds the other visitor. Short stories,
I say. And articles (I mean news, but let him assume
academic). But I haven't finished a novel since
his arrival. There is a solemn silence at this admission.

19 September 2016

The camera distracts me from you.
I become obsessed not with the weight and texture
and noise of this infant but with his image. How
could it possibly be enhanced or over-exposed?
At least the ten beeps and flashing orange light
of the self-timer amuse you while we play together
on the mat. In monochrome I record our eyes
staring into each other's. Your fist is always a happy
blur, my hair is often over my face. I devote
too much time to this task, which makes me feel
sick. Yes, the job is vain, yet it also benefits others –
the baby's great grandmother would appreciate
an envelope of photographs, as would the grand
parents, as would I. So, I spend the precious nap
time uploading and editing. Somehow, seeing you
static on the screen is grim. I think of the radio
interview I listened to about stillborn babies
being dressed and photographed by their parents.

I think about our friend's toddler who fell
from her highchair in the weekend and needed
a craniotomy. I think about the number of
wrong things that could happen to you, whom
I am not tending as well as usual due to the lens.

20 September 2016

What is more important than replying?
You speak with your voice and breath
arms and legs and denim-coloured eyes.
You sound like a cat, a lamb, a piglet, an adult.
You listen, quiet, when I mimic.

21 September 2016

Iris Murdoch said she thought writing
and having a child were quite compatible
activities, mentioning the many examples
of people who manage both. I can't write
these lines (easily) one-handed.
I've had to wait for your eyelids
to drop, to wrap you in a tight swaddle
and place you gentle as an explosive in
your bassinet below the bookshelf on which
spines glow gold with Iris's name.
She also said she wrote everything
by hand – if I were scribbling in my tatty
notebook, I could still be holding you
(who are now emitting choking growls and
hiccups). The green screen (blue these days)
can lull one into finding words too

fascinating to amend, she advised. But
she was working in an era of
conscription and cigarettes and single
copies of manuscripts. Bad art is selfish
fantasy, Iris said. I fear that's what
I'm doing. But there is time to turn it
into pure imagination, to eliminate myself
from the text. The closest to oneness
I have felt is when feeding you and
your soft, sharp fingernails raked
the skin over my ribs and I wondered
if I had grown a third hand.
Here is the problem: how to write
about these months without embroiling
you in a confession that is mine when,
at present, we are not just our separate
selves but also parts of each other. I make
you a son and you make me a mother.

22 September 2016

How many babies have been lullabied
by tinny Beethoven while their parents
hold the line to Centrelink? How many
have been rocked to sleep, lying on
the impatient jiggling thighs of a parent
waiting to ask a Department of Human
Services staff member whether their employer
could exist without Kafka's imagination.
Their computer systems tend to be 'down' or
'out'. An application is 'complete' one day and
the next requires 33% more information.
A 'rental certificate' is demanded by one employee,

but news to another. An automated voice,
which interrupts stringed instruments and
makes your eyelids flicker, says Centrelink
staff will treat me with courtesy and respect,
and that I should endeavour to reciprocate.
I know that I won't when the employee explains
what *accompany* means. You are not listening,
and, It has been six weeks since I submitted
the application, and, Explain what a rental certificate
is and why this is the first I have heard of it. Please
hold the line, the employee replies, and different music
plays, which the baby enjoys as much as the strings
before three beeps tell me the call has failed.

23 September 2016

What are you up to today? asks the handsome café owner
after handing back my credit card. Just strolling? he prompts
my blank face. Yes, I say. Strolling. And so, after sourcing
beans, whole not ground, that puff of dark perfume through the
ventilation holes of their package into my bag, we stroll.
I negotiate the narrow gap between the back of the woman's
chair and the dog bowl full of water. I choose to take a different
route to the shopping strip where I'll buy chicken thighs,
rice, chocolate and butter. Following the railway lines
along South Crescent, I flinch at someone's sculpture –
a life-sized camel head peering over their front fence, realistic
from the neck up, a broomstick from the neck down. I point
out this curiosity to you and vaguely name the plants we pass –
lavender, bougainvillea, rhododendron, daphne, jasmine. I ask
if you can smell spring. Although the air is mild and the sky
clear, I have hidden all but your fat, blotchy face under layers
of wool – purple cardigan, patchwork blanket, cream beanie –

convinced you have a cold. I get us lost in our own suburb.
South Crescent is a dead-end street. A woman in an SUV
tells me: No through road. Back on the familiar south side of
the tracks an elderly cyclist stops and asks me for directions
to Jeffrey Street. I hesitate before answering, not trusting myself.
You're confused too, he says pleasantly. I refrain from telling him
that I live near Jeffrey Street and know exactly where it is, but am
simply collecting my thoughts. Eventually I provide what I think
are unambiguous directions and his bony Lycra legs pedal off
uncertainly, leaving us to continue. When we reach Station Street
and the shops, Cancer Council collectors with white smiles,
I assume but do not see, accost me. How's it going today?
a young man asks, sidling up with his clipboard and sticky tone.
I am extremely tired, I say.

24 September 2016

A friend who is a father asks
if there has been an epiphany.
We are at the Merri Table at CERES,
waiting for bacon and eggs after
a group run, in which I walked
with a pram. My parents have that
pram containing my son. They are
pushing it alongside the brown
frothy creek or around the market
stalls selling homemade toddler
pinafores, fair-trade chocolate, bio
dynamic vegetables, free-range
eggs and environmentally friendly
glitter. Past the sign telling dog
owners to steer clear of the hens.
I am too distracted with imagining

where the baby in the grey-and-white
striped suit and purple cardigan
could be. Did my mother feel this
distraction? Presumably she does not
feel it still. No, I say, no epiphany.

25 September 2016

We walk without talking.
We read without talking.
We eat lunch with few words.
We talk to and about you.
When I go downstairs to the bathroom,
I hear you talking to each other.
When, I wonder, did this silence set in?
Has it always been there? Did I cause it
by describing us in an old poem as
a quiet family. Not too quiet I hope, Mum wrote
in an email. We text instead of call.
We apologise[15] a lot. I even stop
talking to you as much, until they leave

---

15 To Regret
All of my emails were beginning with apologies – *I'm sorry for not writing back sooner* – until
you warned against guilt and I asked you what you had been guilty about. Ignoring your own
mother and personal failings, you mentioned – alcohol, cigarettes. But, above all, not giving
me a much craved sibling. You offered excuses – your depression, my father's back surgery,
your age. And at last it was easy to say a kind thing – a true thing – to you. That my childhood
was idyllic even (or perhaps due to being) without brother or sister. I convince myself of this
idyll often now, while our friends stoically make siblings for their children. This is all for her, a
pregnant friend referred to her daughter. There is no benefit for the parents in having a second
child – it's all for the first. Such words are a flippant dismissal of the deeply felt, similar to *I
hate being pregnant* and *I hope it won't be a boy* – phrases that I couldn't reply to during the
year of barren waiting. Writing was replaced with waiting. Waiting came to feel like wasting.
All of it wanting.

for a walk up High Street. Please, I say
to you, while I slice a leek with you strapped
to my chest and butting my breast
gently with your nose. Please, don't
let this silence spread down into
the next layer of my family.

26 September 2016

It's a geometric existence
pacing a golden circle around
the living room, estimating
the angle of your eyelids,
begging it to decrease
until the lashes are tucked
inside a calm sleeping line,
counting hours and collecting
data, observing your shape change,
the asymptotic thigh creases
deepen with each week.

27 September 2016

The cry is different
deeper and rawer,
a roar as sudden and urgent
as the needle in the thigh.
The second cry overlaps
and negates the first.
It is voiceless with disbelief.
The world is turning
into a sharp and unreliable

place where pain and
horrible tastes and
vomit and cold hands
and light in the eyes,
instruments in the ears,
stick in the mouth,
heavy disc on the back
and front, listening to
what is keeping you alive
are commonplace as
milk once was. Your first
feed after the ordeal
is hesitant and suspicious.
You have every reason
to believe the nipple is
full of sweet venom.
For most of the afternoon
you sleep and make
the usual farmyard
grunts and hisses.
This time I listen
for fever dreams.

28 September 2016

Rosie the hairdresser has a new fringe.
Her dog, Buddy, is absent today.
A friend of a friend has just had a cut
and is putting an anorak on
her toddler, who examines the plastic
animals arranged on a shelf.
I am out without you, I am out
of the house. Rosie asks how

are things. Usually she compliments me
on my hair. Not this time. In the large
mirror I am a strange colour
around the eyes. What do I want
done, she asks. Short, as short as possible,
I say, meaning as short as will look okay.
A blunt bob is addictive, isn't it, she says,
snipping already at my dry hair. It's like,
she says, a good hat that you don't even
have to put on. It's just always there.
Yes. She understands that I can't
have colour today – that would take
too long. It's the first time I have left
you in your six weeks of life. An hour
is more than enough solitude. Rosie makes me
a pot of peppermint tea and gossips softly
about people I know and washes my hair
with something that smells of almonds
and geranium leaf and massages my scalp
until I'm afraid I'll fall asleep.
Rosie is much smaller than me.
If I lost consciousness with my head
in the basin, there I would stay.

29 September 2016

I can't hug my mother goodbye
properly because I am holding you.
She puts a lean arm
around my waist, squeezes and
says something kind about
my parenting. I want to hold her.
When my father hugs me goodbye,

you are squashed between us
and in this moment you, miraculous,
fall asleep, after hours of pacing
and patting. All your fuss has been
smothered. You sleep
for five hours in a row – a new
record. Whether it is the smell
of your grandparents' adoration or
the sensation of your mother relaxing
after a week of visitors, I do not know.
'Visitors'[16] is harsh and incorrect.
My parents sat silently reading and
completing crossword after crossword,
speaking in whispers when spoken to,
which was seldom. They trudged in
single file, in a Melbourne downpour,
behind me pushing the pram from the GP's
clinic; they bought pasta sauce and lasagne
for us to put in the freezer and gave us
space, going to an Ethiopian restaurant
for their own dinner. Anxiously
they tried to pack the dishwasher as we do,
to find the right places to put things.
And, when I went to get my hair cut,
they cared for you for an hour and a half,
letting me return to a quiet, peaceful
house and to you, who wanted feeding.
No, not visitors, barely people, so familiar

16 To Visit
Perhaps it's right after all. The origin of visit implies a call paid by those with a particular power
to see, examine or inspect – gods, pastors, doctors. Except, these visitors were not judgemental
and they offered no diagnosis. They did not want merely to see but to hold. Within seconds of
the baby waking, my father had laid the little parcel of progeny across his long, strong forearm.

and loaded with meaning they are almost
symbols and I wish I didn't see them in this
way and hope you will not see the origins
of the parts of yourself you like least in me;
will not wait until the last minute to be
kind, to be grateful, to be generous.
As they leave, my husband pats the small
of my back, realising before I do that
the parting is hard. We're not
a demonstrative family, but we love
each other deeply is what the upset means,
I finally understand as tears rise and
fall while I walk you who have woken
briefly before sinking again into sleep.

30 September 2016

A still, sleeping child's vest
undulating subtly above
his breath is a relief.

1 October 2016

Was it wrong to bring the baby
to a Grand Final party? I could have
predicted how the roars of triumph
and despair would affect his seven-
week-old limbs. The startle reflex
opened him up with every mark,
even when I held the soft white
rag we use to mop milk from
his mouth over his ears to

protect him from voices –
his father's, his parents'
friends' – raised not in
real emotion, but in such
a good likeness that his
instinctive fear kicked in.
The only way to explain this
behaviour is to show him. While
the game plays out, I feed my baby
and help a five-year-old make a Lego
truck and caravan. The boy smiles
shyly at the adults' yells, understanding
not their purpose but their connection
to the green field and red and blue figures
hurtling into each other. When he sees
the baby flinch at a collective cry he seems
to want to pat the younger person's head
and say, It will be all right.

2 October 2016

The poems are gradually slowing, like
the blood, the lochia. I think it's over
and then wake to find a new stain on the
paper, surprisingly bright and wonder
where it came from exactly (wound or
waste?) and why. Ought I worry?

The baby is emitting pained sounds
except when drinking from my breast
or lying over my shoulder and having
a large hand drum soothing rhythms
or stroke soothing circles on his back.

My palm hums calmly – the rubbing's
energy working on me at least. And,
now he has dropped off the breast
like a windfall.

3 October 2016

While feeding you today I read a poetry collection
full of similes. Everything is like something else
unexpected, often from another era. It is a sort of
creativity to place two existing things together and
to notice how different they make everything look.
You claw at me like anxiety,[17] regret, anger or

---

17 To Abstract

In his essay 'On Abstraction', Brian Blanchfield shares his conviction that there are 'spirits, *numina*, in language' – these imbue words with value and ensure that even abstract nouns have a tangible quality. When he lists obvious abstracts (love, peace, flight, desire, terror, symmetry, death, appetite, doubt), I feel that squirming uncertainty I (shouldn't, but do) hide when teaching linguistics, about the distinction between concrete and abstract nouns. The way in which I understand each of the words in the parenthesised list above is based on tangible experiences – bodily reactions and sensations.

In a sort of symmetrical agreement with Brian, I would suggest that concrete nouns (milk, blood, water, sleep, breast, teeth, tongue) possess an intangible, abstract quality too – they function as ideas as well as solid forms or states of being. Is this notion just a bodily version of William Carlos Williams's 'no ideas but in things'? I wonder whether I would feel less furtive and inhibited, more proud and academic, if the repeated concrete nouns in this journal were conventionally abstract. Yes, she is exposing her body – worse still, her baby's body and her husband's – but what does it mean? What must it mean? If only it were more abstract. In the epistemology unit of Year 11 Philosophy we talk about a mathematician's challenging of what it means to *know* non-Euclidean geometry. If one can crochet hyperbolic space, does one know? Do coral understand what they embody? Might the rhythms of mouth sucking, slippers padding, stainless-steel barrel turning and slapping its wet contents, waking and sleeping mean that something is being kept alive?

It has been a struggle to return to this document today, after reading excerpts from and interviews with the author of a recently published collection of poems also recounting experiences of early motherhood. I haven't read the whole book yet. I know I should, and I know it's foolish to feel as if what I'm writing and editing has already been said. I worry that

envy, distracting me from all other thoughts and
activities. When you sleep, I want to sleep too, as if
our eyelids were on the same timer. I am quite unlike
the poet of this book, but her words
describe things exactly as I have experienced them,
like orgasms, like longing, like fear, like hatred.
Normally I would not write such words in case
they leaked into reality. This poet makes wet
black flowers spill out of a telephone receiver;
this is what I see when my eyes drift away
carried on sleep. This is what disappears when the
child cries out, demanding undivided reading.

the meaning of this journal stops at the body – the subject, the phenomenon. That beyond the 'pity the martyr, the tired new mother, and admire her sanctity, her love and care for the infant' implication, the content of the journal is absent and thus any other work on the topic could leave this manuscript redundant. Abstractly, I believe this is not true, but my bodily reaction is of fight or flight.

Originally, the verb 'to abstract' meant to draw away from or remove. Later, it meant to consider something as a general idea without regard to matter. The matter, I want to say, is humming with meaning, just as Blanchfield sees the meaning of certain nouns as material with value. The matter that, I want to say, is typically feminine – blood, milk, urine, food, drink, sheets, towels – tends to couple with verbs; there is an infinite amount to do, which is what led me to start titling these footnotes with infinitives.

Assumptions that doing and thinking are exclusive – that abstract thought, which draws the thinker away from the action or matter of the subject – may lead to a view that abstraction is a more serious, cerebral occupation than the matters of washing and feeding. This was an assumption I made ten years ago. When deciding on a critical lens through which to analyse the contemporary epic poem for my PhD thesis, I subconsciously eschewed a feminist reading, wanting to cast myself as an ambitious academic, willing and able to ignore her own gender and the domesticity, deceptive narrowness and concreteness it risked saturating the study in. It is an assumption I have to remind myself not to make when considering this journal as an embarrassing waste of time, a record of bodily waste. Mere matter. When the front of the journal in which I recorded Robin's vital statistics (sleep, feeds, nappy changes) and the back in which I wrote these entries met in the middle, I was frustrated that the raw data of the baby's matter was intruding on what I hoped was poetry. But the writing that remains here can read just as tediously and earthily as the crooked columns of record-keeping. It all matters.

4 October 2016

Again, there was an idea and again it has gone
for want of a pen, paper, spare right hand, will.
Write about this, you tell yourself, when his
hind legs bend like a frog's and his feet thump
your stomach and his fingernails, which you've
tried to file smooth, scratch at your neck and
his voice grizzles, and you tell him, It's all right,
without knowing whether it is, and, I know
what you want, without knowing at all, just
assuming it is hunger or wind or overtiredness.
What if he is trying to escape the world, to climb
into a place he remembers better than you do,
but still only faintly? You think of the television
programme you've just watched in which a superhuman
child tears a hole in space and time. The portal
is viscous, part spiderweb, part vagina; to pass
from one world to its mirror image takes
the sort of force the baby exerts when he scrabbles
up your torso. The noises he makes resemble those
the powerful child emits when her nose bleeds
and she breaks an adult's neck telekinetically.

5 October 2016

You need a passport photo. The man at the post shop looks into the
pram and says, No, too tiny, sorry. He directs me to a narrow alleyway
a few doors down the street. I wheel the pram past a succulent in a
large pot and find an overgrown back lawn and a rickety flight of steps
to an abode. There is a sign at the bottom of the steps saying *Photoart*,
and another blowing across the long grass saying *Back at 12:30*. I look
at my watch and see the hands sitting at 12:30 (it is 11:30), so we set

about ascending the homemade staircase. Curled into a comma and covered in an eggplant-coloured cardigan, you really are little. I could be clutching a garment to my chest. Up the stairs, leaving the pram in the strange backyard, we're stuck in a sort of glass ante-room. The door to the dwelling has another sign – *Back in 10 mins*. Next to this door is an open window, through which I discern a dark little kitchen with a kettle on the stovetop. In the waiting area, there are stacks of canvases printed with pretend people – a bride too young and calm for it to be a real wedding day; a couple on a beach. In the far corner is a stand of greeting cards, faded to pale blue and curling at the edges. *Get a drink in ya*, says one, above a frothy pint. Another is of a Transformer. I wonder whether the photographer expected to be back at 12:30 (or in ten minutes) today, or several decades ago.

6 October 2016

It is a spring day that feels like summer in Hawke's Bay.
I have bare legs and all the windows open. When we walked
home from Clifton Hill, workers were cutting the grass
verges, bright sparks of green flying in a cloud around them.
They stopped courteously as the pram passed, letting us
walk through a quiet haze of that fresh pea smell. I want
you to feel grass on your feet, so I take you to the park
after lunch and roll up the aqua-striped foot mittens of
your suit and position you on the quilt as if it were the edge
of a swimming pool, your fat feet, unused to air or light
let alone clover and oxalis, dabbling in a new texture.
Like our bath together last night, this moment is one
I had imagined would last longer, each of us languid and
relishing. But, being placed on a small quilt in the middle
of a meadow, with the main road flowing to the north,
a brown creek with burst banks to the west,
a track carrying dog-walkers, runners and cyclists to the east,

a tree of swooping magpies – their young squeaking like toys –
to the south, and aeroplanes above is too much.
Somehow you realise your size and status in this scene.
The only thing to do is suck your knuckles and kick
your drumstick legs. In kicking, your soles are
tickled with cool, papery strands of something new and
your fist is released, it relaxes back into a hand and your lips,
instead of sucking grimly, stretch into a helpless smile.

7 October 2016

The falls are engorged and the colour
of old coffee. We are alone at the lookout.
I put the brake on the pram and step back
to take a photo of you so close to the bellowing,
scummy water, then a step forward to inspect it
myself, as if you weren't here. An onlooker might
find my behaviour strange, I think. But that
in itself is a strange thought. It's a relief
to know that what I'm sensing has been
named by the French – *l'appel du vide*.

8 October 2016

Sheep are the granite sculptures of the sun.
Oxalis paints the fields yellow.
The baby stretches out his fingers and groans
when the car gives way.
The sky is a hot, honest blue, with only two
milk stains of cloud. This is his
first visit to Longwood.

*

So satisfying, my husband says
with a large dandelion in his hands,
its rhizome of roots clinging
to a clod of earth. It is indeed,
I think from my position on the sofa,
baby over my shoulder, a breeze
on my face and ankles, a view of purple
hibiscus, rust-red wheelbarrow,
and the two friends working.
I feel like the woman in the Truman Capote
story I've just started reading, who
lies about having been to the south
and has too many sailors at her soirée.
At least these weeds have the decency
to grow upwards, not like this ground cover
that doesn't really grow, but oozes.
My husband's words and the brilliant
white band of lower back exposed
when he bends to the task make me
smile. Usually I'd be out there among
the succulents and parrots, the flies and
sunshine. There's dirt under my fingernails
from this morning's gentle effort in the vege
garden, but my primary job now is letting the fat
warm creature sleep over my shoulder. We need
an auxiliary plan. I feel like America going into Iraq.
This speaker is our friend. What to do once the bed
is cleared, to stop the weeds from simply returning?
Straw is too messy. He thinks perhaps pebbles.
Yes, but we don't have any pebbles, my husband replies.
Our friend says it's all right; his mother's coming
to visit next week. In a car? Yes. I wonder whether
the milk-dead weight on my chest, snoring quietly,

will ever call and request that I bring a bag of
ornamental pebbles for him. I would put the sleeping
baby down on the makeshift bed (quilt on sheepskin
on floor) and join the labourers. But I'm enjoying
the weight of him – a contented weight that will
twitch and flinch when separated from my skin.
There will be plenty of separation to come.
Look at all that, just from one root! Our friend waves
a small shrub in triumph. Once he would've chased

such a line with, That's what she said. But
now the roots mean only what they are –
the conduit of nutrients between soil and
plant – and remind me vaguely of why we went in
on this property despite owning nothing else. This foolish
expense will be tenacious as a weed? The simile isn't
satisfactory but the idea persists. One day, the baby
will be a child who kneels and weeds and learns
more than we know now about the soil and how
to distinguish between weeds and the plants we want.
What if, I wondered, looking at Alison Lester's illustrations
of things parents want to give their child – a cosy bedroom
with a view of a tree full of wattlebirds; a garden rippling
with tulips and roses; a perfectly weeded vegetable patch
with benign insects for a child to discover; friendly cats,
dogs and horses; a rock pool full of rainbow-coloured fish;
a koala above us in a tree; a woollen blanket and a steaming
mug of tea at the fireside. What if we never have a garden?
Or pets. Or perfect holidays. At least he will know
that we wished such pleasures would be his. This book
is a petitionary prayer of sorts, and I realise now
that the answer to these requests is here, dilapidated
and overgrown and snake-infested, but here.

9 October 2016

I explain to you that you should be sleeping,
that I am writing. I ask you whether you can
sleep. You shake your head and I'm charmed
by this coincidence. I count to three and hoist you
from bassinet to arms, letting your face stare back
over my right shoulder. Now you are really awake,

I take you to the kitchen and help myself to
the jellybeans in the loud plastic bag, which I'd
not dared to raid half an hour ago.
Having eaten three lollies, all yellow, all
tasting faintly of Lemsip and Strepsils, I walk
past the glass-fronted print by a New Zealand
artist of a lonesome white bungalow on a hill
behind a black railway track. In the glass's
reflection, your eyes are shut. I perform
the move that is working so far, bending at the
waist as I lower you into the crib, keeping my chest
against you until your back has touched the mattress
and we must separate, at which you always squirm,
deprived however gradually of the warmth we've made.
I keep my palms under your own tiny spine and shoulders,
sliding them out gingerly, as I'd slide paper
under a glass containing a spider. When we split
in two, your face has a dark pink crease across
the cheek, where the fold of my sweatshirt has been.

Back at the laptop I read through the weeks of
words herded into fifteen-minute corrals, fenced in
between sleeps – both mine and yours. Some lines,
clearly, are escaping through this barrier – half in,
half out of consciousness. Dreamily liminal. I read

backwards until I reach the document's working
title, *Neonatal*. Too clinical to be appropriate now,
I play with the cursor, like the baby plays with the
nipple when he wants comfort rather than food.
I keep *Neon*: a bright, new, elemental word
like a swipe of highlighter over these days
in the calendar. I add *Days*, then change it
to *Daze*. This is where I am, in a floodlit
stupor, so bright I can barely see, like in Dante's
Paradise, shadowless knowledge so pure it's empty.[18]

10 October 2016

The teacher, Rachel, tells the mothers to relax
their big bones, followed by their small bones,
their big muscles, followed by their small muscles,
their big organs, followed by their small organs.
The biggest organ, she tells us, is the skin. We must
relax our physical skins. Then, we must consider
our other kinds of skin – our mental and emotional
and spiritual skins. I am imagining torn clingfilm,
and feeling the baby's sharp heels kick against the
physical skin of my shoulder. I know mine is a bad
savasana or dead body pose, as I am stroking my son's
tummy and fat, kicking thighs, trying to stop him
calling out during Rachel's monologue. She blows
bubbles and fills the studio with quivering rainbow
spheres for the babies to admire while their mothers'

---

18 To Doubt
Doubt comes from *duo*, which comes from *two*, in the sense of two minds, undecided. To
include this explanatory note or not? (Is it a darling to kill, or just a darling? Because I do not
know, I do not kill – *stet*. Let it stand.)

eyes are closed. Your baby is safe and well, relax,
Rachel repeats. Your baby is safe and well, relax.

11 October 2016

First socks (white with navy fish), first
dance to '(I've Had) The Time of My Life',
first listening to Can's 'Vitamin C'
(to which you fell peacefully asleep),
first passport. A friend comes for morning
tea and signs the backs of two photos
of your swift little face – it took the Australia
Post man thirty attempts to get a shot
that would comply with the Department of
Immigration and Citizenship's standards.
This afternoon, we will deliver the paperwork
back to the post office and wait three weeks
for the leather-covered book that you'll keep
for five years. Will you look anything like yourself
by then? Today I saw a photo of the North Island
robin, toutouwai; in its grey wings, white chest,
and small handsomeness, I saw you – this is
who you are named after, not Robin Hood, not
even Christopher Robin, really, you are the
creature described on the Department of
Conservation website as friendly, trusting and
possessing a strong, descending, repetitive call.

12 October 2016

Are you going to talk to me, darling?
the nurse asks and your cooing
reply makes me inordinately proud.
The rattle passes left to right
across your face and the two pāua-
green eyes follow its path. The nurse
asks if your stare is always straight
and I, convinced you are perfect,
admit that your pupils cross slightly
when you are tired. This is a flaw
to be observed and, if not outgrown
in the next two months, a reason
to send you to an optometrist.
My pride is not diminished; only,
a corner of it is now obscured by
worry, by a picture of a toddler
wearing heavy glasses, of a boy
with a Labrador in a harness.
Amblyopia (a lazy, or ambling eye)
or strabismus (a squint), your father
tells us, is fairly common and easily treated.
You may wear an eyepatch. Now
my pride is patterned with pirate ships.

3

13 October 2016

After exactly two months in mostly
your company, mainly on our couch,
listening to little but my own voice
making sounds rather than words, while
wearing the same sweatshirt, trackpants
and nursing singlets day after day,
I am on a stage opposite a grand piano.
A young man is playing Chopin.
To my right is the professor of surgery,
to my left a lectern with two small
microphones. Behind me sits a pastor,
and three medical students holding
short speeches on pieces of A4 paper.
In my lap is my own contribution –
a poem in ten-point font, so as to fit
on one side (turning a page seemed
disrespectful on such an occasion).
The professor speaks first
about his courage as an equestrian
and a surgeon, about the need to give
bad news to patients. These anecdotes
are linked tenuously to the sacrifice made
by family members of the seven hundred
people in the audience. I watch the faces
listen to the anatomy student describe
a tendon as never just dull white but
both silver and gold. A woman wipes
her eyes. A child in a tuxedo squirms free
and crawls under his seat. I try not to look
out the long wall of windows down the east
side of the hall for the pram. I hear a faint
cry and feel my breasts stretch with milk.

Usually, I would be heated with nerves,
my heart thumping every other organ,
but this time the shyness is diffuse and
strange. I sympathise with you, newborn,
overwhelmed by unfamiliar sounds and
smells. In my public appearance outfit
I am not sure I am even myself – instead,
I seem to be holidaying in a previous life,
which is usually only possible via dreams.
I hate extemporising, but realise, while
the pianist plays Liszt before I am due
to read my poem, that I must say something
introductory. Ordinarily I would have written
a sentence or two and tried to read it casually,
but now I must memorise. Honour or privilege?
How not to stumble, as I inevitably do over
unrehearsed words? This is oneiric because
it's only in the shower and in my dreams that
I am not holding the boy. Because of the surreal
audience. Because of the way the words fall
into almost perfect sentences and the poem[19]

19 To Donate
To turn one's body into a gift to be opened is to decide that you belong to no one but yourself.
The family of a donor suffers the loss of a funeral, as its relative's remains must be transported
immediately to the university. In the film shown during an ethics lecture to undergraduate
medical students, a woman explains that when her husband died, she stopped walking past the
university because knowing his body was inside somewhere, in some form, was too upsetting.
I am forbidden from referring, in the poem, to specific defining features of the bodies I see
when – green gown draped wide over eight months' pregnant stomach – I observe a dissection
class. No mention of toenail polish, for instance. Look, an excited student with scarlet gloves
says, this is a massive spleen. He starts to pass me the organ before realising I am a civilian
with naked hands. The poem is a gift to the families, who require elegy and information. They
want to know how their parent's or sibling's or spouse's body was indispensable. It is tempting
to rely on stale consolations – the person is not their body; they feel no incisions. But that is
to understate the power of the lived-in skin. There is nothing like a real person who has lived.

winds like a mobile; after the effort of the first
few lines, the rest is just music and turning
shapes. Like the mobile it stops abruptly
and there is a silence before sombre applause.

14 October 2016

As the recent Nobel Prize–winner sings
Hey, Mr Tambourine Man
you wake with a yell, so I wash olive oil
off my hands and go straight to you, kissing
your rash-red cheeks and receiving a small
smile. You will remember the year that Dylan
won as the year of your birth, the month as
the second of your life, full of wisteria, jasmine
and viburnum. The day as the day that your mother
tried to loosen the mucus in your nostrils with
a saline drop that made you squeal and vomit
with outrage, looking her in the eye through
your new tears shining with total betrayal.

15 October 2016

It's like being in the front row at the theatre,
crossing at the lights just as the body I'd noticed
from the car a few days ago starts his electronic
playlist before sprinting the one hundred metres
around the burnt umber track. Spring sun brings
out the rubbery scent of the surface his shoes are
pounding. Aside from shoes and black shorts,
he is otherwise exposed, shaped from sweat and
light and however many reps he does each day.

Behind my sunglasses, I stare as he collapses into
a child's posture, folded at the knees and hips, arms
stretched out as if in supplication. Hearing
someone else's breath is intimate. His reminds me
of an essay I read recently about a woman who's
decided to no longer hide her puffing when riding
a bike uphill or at the tail end of a run. The man,
only metres from the pram, a heaving lump of
breathing flesh, seems to be performing. What am I
supposed to feel? Loose and swingy about the thighs,
stiff-hipped, slightly too hot and thirsty despite
dawdling. Across the road, a woman is jogging slowly
and steadily, with ropy thighs and a sense of purpose.
Under the bridge, the Merri Creek is a muscle
tanned and flexed with rain. It seems that we alone, baby,
are the soft parts of this scene, unfit for our first summer.

16 October 2016

The Bureau of Meteorology radar is stained
dark blue with yellow and red in the centre,
like a Mondrian creme egg, which suggests
it's going to absolutely pour in the next few
minutes, but we have driven all this way and
even if it's not been picnic weather, we must
at least climb to the summit of the rock. You are
strapped to your father's front and zipped under
his red jacket. I cover your head with a grey hat.
Our friends, usually intrepid, are reluctant
to stray far from the cars, but your father insists
that we quickly follow the path to the top. It is,
he assures everyone, an easy walk. He's forgotten
that the path gives way to mossy boulders.

From behind, no one would know he was carrying
you. I follow his footsteps exactly, as if repeating
them makes them firmer and will stop any slipping.
I am a mountain goat, our friend says;
he has another friend's one-year-old strapped
to his front. I have seen you fall, your father replies.
And I think it has something to do with you thinking
you are a mountain goat. The words are said tensely
as he holds his left arm around you and balances
with his right palm against a rock. The sky is
granite too – shimmering, hard and slick.

17 October 2016

Like school, like a conference, like any situation
involving me and others, I wait a few metres away
from the group, hiding behind the pram, talking
only to you, until (like at school, like at conferences)
some kind extrovert approaches and introduces
herself. I join the corner with the other mothers
who've chosen unisex names for their children.
This is Marlowe, she says. It goes with her plaid
shirt, black jeans and Raybans. This is Robin, I reply.
Marlowe is a girl, she says. Robin is a boy, I say.
Soon, Pax joins our babies on the northwest side
of the circle. We strip the infants down to nappies
and rub a fruity massage oil on our palms. Today
we learn a new relaxation technique. Marlowe screams
at the first touch of her mother's shiny fingers.
Cold hands? the nurse asks. Marlowe's mother
lets her daughter leave the fragrant circle
and returns to a chair to breastfeed. I am left to
compare Robin's rolly thighs and round belly

with Pax's. The purpose of this group is primarily
comparison, I realise late. Next week will be devoted
to 'ages and stages'. I learn not to mention six
hours' sleep in a row or babbling that sounds
like talking. It's best to complain – anything else
seems smug. Marlowe's mother goes to the changing
room, and Pax's paces about, swinging him to sleep.
I am left sitting alone with you in the pram,
now dozing too; the nurse-convenor takes pity
and keeps me company. I should introduce myself
to the louder parents of children named after flowers;
this must be how it begins – perhaps my mother
lurked at the edges of our playgroup and I absorbed
her nervous watchfulness. Next week I will show you
how to socialise. More likely, you will show me.

18 October 2016

Today is my birthday. The baby's had his first
bowel movement in five days and is now sleeping.
I eat lunch in the sun and watch a video of a kiwi
hatching from an egg already cracked and held
in place with masking tape until the chick was ready
to emerge. His pink beak and sharp, wet feathers
are evident before anything like a whole body or
face can be identified. His innate knowledge of
how to thrust his face forward and twist like a
squeezed sponge, wringing out a previous
contained life's liquid and readying himself –
lighter and drier – for a new existence is easy
to confuse with bravery or grit or any admirable
quality that suggests a choice in the matter,
an understanding of his precarious position.

He is slick with newness and clean of any blame;
perhaps it's this purity rather than grit which
inflates something that feels like a billowing pillow
case of my lungs or long shadow cast by my ribcage
or fat doppelgänger heart. Really, I guess it's just
breath, just air, nothing more than what that kiwi
is learning to breathe, and what made you squawk.

19 October 2016

I do not care if the toys and furniture are all wooden
and Danish. I do not care for the award-winning
music programme. I do not care for the organic lunches
and the daily photos emailed through. I care that
it is eight minutes' jog from where I will probably
be working next year. I care that it takes babies
four months younger than you will be, so must
be accustomed to tiny children and grieving, sleep-
deprived mothers. Little do you know that in three
and a half months, there will be a wrenching
severance[20] each morning. Little did I know
even adding your name to a waiting list would hurt.

20 To Sever
'Sever' derives from the Latin *separare*, whose morphemes mean 'apart' (*se*) and 'make ready
or prepare' (*parare*). We are getting ready to be apart. If only this writing self could have told
the self walking around the double-fronted cottage converted into a daycare centre that, a
year later, the rooms that seemed dangerously full of the mess and business of other people's
toddlers would be bright during the black mornings of midwinter. As the days shorten, the
7am drop-off will be clouded with warm breath. I will point to the silhouetted hot-air balloons
(and gradually you will too) before entering the code, walking down the corridor lined with
toddlers' paintings, and passing you to a carer. Bernadette and Nancy, Steph and Steph,
Katerina and Bree, Caitlin and Nathan, Rebecca and Harrison, Ling and Reuben, the people
who initially look too young and distracted to be trusted with you, will become your adult
friends and surrogate parents. In the first week you will be cuddled close to Bernadette's polo

20 October 2016

It's fortunate that I have a template already replete
with lyrical bragging about someone I don't resemble
currently but must have passed for once; someone
who writes whole books and edits and teaches, who does
cerebral tasks, whose feet don't spend the majority of
each day sliding over the living-room floorboards in
a sleepy circle, whose palms pat an Ethiopian rhythm
on your nappy and back, who can go a whole day
without noticing the wet, rancid stain leaking through
her singlet to her sweatshirt. Mine should be called
a milk shirt. I hear a woman on the news say
something has been 'secreted away', reminding me of
the satisfying opposition between 'secret' and 'secrete'.
Like stress balls, I roll these words around my
echoing mind, then throw in 'precede' and 'proceed'.
The first pair is red, the second yellow, the third –
'discrete' and 'discreet' – blue. The surface is a
green baize cloth with a black triangle mould.
When the baby cries, all the balls sink together.
I like this metaphor so much I fear I might
table it during the job interview, as evidence
(surely) that I am more than arms, breasts, face –
more important than comfort, food and knowledge.

shirt, wide eyes tracking me leaving in tears. Then you will take your low seat at the toddler table and be given two squares of toast. Sometimes you will grizzle in ritual imitation of the other children, or in genuine sorrow at our parting. But because we have prepared – because we have been cut from each other early – the time apart will become as easy as any habit. When I return in the afternoons, I'll find you digging in the sandpit with a spoon and a small frying pan, serious in your lone task. Robin, I say. You look at me with a half smile and I sit on the edge of the pit, next to you. After a few more spoonfuls into the pan you are ready. Arms up. Time to go home now? Nod.

21 October 2016

Today, a neonatologist came to afternoon tea.
She brought strawberries and giant chocolate
macarons and translated your facial expressions
and coos into words, for example: Tired eyes now,
Mum. Usually, this subtitling of my child
would irk, but she seems to know, like a horse
whisperer, like Temple Grandin, the savant whom
abattoirs employed to test whether their floor plans
were humane – if the cows knew their fate before
they turned the corner. At home, Grandin kept
a hugging machine for when she craved arms
but could not tolerate the intensity of another
person. I am not good at hugging and kissing
adults in greeting – I never know whether to do so
or not and would really prefer that everyone simply
shook hands – but I love hugging babies and children.
I touch you and you touch[21] me more than anyone else
these days. Websites warn that mothers' libidos wane
not just due to hormones but because mothers are so full
to the brim with affection given to and received from
their baby that they have no need for more intimacy.

21 **To Touch**
I bet no one has touched your ears more often than me, said Rosie the hairdresser when I last
saw her. She wishes she could detach and reattach them, to avoid the fiddly snipping. The words
came after a long, not awkward lack of conversation between us. They were weird, intimate and
right; they could, I thought in the moment I was due to give a reply, stand for our relationship.
You or Robin – the competition would be close, I think I told her, or at least thought.

22 October 2016

The one-year-old cousin is wearing a wolf costume.
His wolf head is removed when his birthday cupcake
comes. He has never had chocolate before and winces
slightly at the first bite, before slamming the lump of
ganache in the vicinity of his mouth and grinning.
The blond-haired, blue-eyed boy has given himself
a delightful Hitler moustache. Everybody claps.

23 October 2016

Your grandmother has started attending the museum
in preparation for showing you the taxidermied Phar Lap
and reconstructed dinosaur skeletons. She tells us about
a manic small boy whose mother apologised, saying he isn't
always like that; he is just excited. She clearly wants you to be
that boy one day soon, your legs and tongue running, running
from exhibit to exhibit, hungrily learning as your father did.

24 October 2016

Today, as we pace around the room, I compare
you with animals and birds and eventually
I decide to try writing a picture book that is
as good as *Hello, Baby*, if not quite as good as
Where Is the Green Sheep? I am happy to report
that you enjoyed my final draft of this attempt, so,
buoyed with vain optimism, I sent the manuscript
to Penguin.[22] Here, in case it never sees the light of day,
is my text:

A Curious Bird

You are a curious bird, bright as a flame robin.
You wriggle and squirm acting the worm

when the morning is dark as a magpie lark.
You giggle with your mother like a kookaburra,

and she beams at you like an emu. At dawn
you bellow like a crimson rosella, merry as a cassowary.

Watchful as a bulbul, at noon you coo
like a cockatoo and your squeal is a cockatiel's.

You drink like a parched zebra finch, flap and flail
like Willie Wagtail, and float like a charm of pardalotes.

At night you are sweeter than a honeyeater
and finer than a noisy miner

when (more superb than a fairy wren)
you yawn and sigh, sleepy as a nest of silvereyes.

22 To Cringe

The Proto-Germanic origin (*krank*) means to bend or curl up, as one would when being beaten, to protect the vital organs from damage, or when cold, embryonic, ashamed, or in pain. Keep it inside, safe, protected from rejection, from cursory attention, from unkind scrutiny is the impulse, but the other urge is to unfurl, expose, publish. Why? Is it right to include this private piece of writing, whose audience was at the time two months old? If not, then where to draw the line? There are many entries in this journal that I think are sloppy (sentimental and imprecise) poetry, but which seem at times to be alive with a crucial value. A little like the scribbles he makes; it's difficult to imitate a toddler's uninhibited drawing style – my lines are too heavy and sure or confected cobwebs. I don't draw a line, Bornholdt said, referring to the zone of appropriateness when writing about one's family. There is no line like one dragged across brown cardboard Booktopia packaging by a dimpled fist. All lines should stand alone beautifully, my PhD supervisor told me, paraphrasing Olsen or Simic. What is the first thing

25 October 2016

Strange to be on the balcony looking at a bleached
sky and hearing, from downstairs, heavy rain
on an ocean and thunder, and through the storm
no yelps or cries or breath, just weather.

26 October 2016

We are two-thirds of the way through a long walk and the clouds[23] are
dense and we find ourselves in the Darling Gardens, approaching a
rotunda in which two people argue. Or, rather, one man who sounds
like he wants his next fix – do you say *fix* or *hit*, I don't know – of ice
is berating a silent woman, who stares at her feet. I am the good guy
here, don't treat me like the bad guy, he repeats, sounding like a bad
guy. His tone wakes you and makes you cry. Really, you are hungry,
but he doesn't know that. He pauses briefly in his rant, but doesn't look
at us – it is as if he has heard the baby's cry but doesn't know where it
is from; as if we exist on a separate plane from his fight. I wheel you as
fast as I can across the grass, away from the rotunda, to a park bench
that doesn't have beer cans underneath it, where I can lift up my top
in relative comfort and feed you. If you were not here, would I have

that comes to mind when you read this word? I ask, writing *line* on the board in a linguistics
class. A cringe is a curved line that reminds me of a koru or fern frond – a beautiful thing.

23 To Name
Yesterday on the radio there was an interview with a man who'd written a book about clouds.
Luke Howard, a nineteenth-century pharmacist with an interest in clouds, is responsible for
the lovely Latin names that click together like pieces of Lego, according to the interviewer.
Cumulus – heap; cirrus – curl of hair; cumulocirrus – heap of curls of hair? Howard named the
clouds so well that Goethe wrote him a letter of congratulations. A common misconception is
that clouds float, when really they are in a constant slow descent. During our last flight, your
nose pressed the cold window, eyes as close as possible to the changing whites and blues. So
many names to teach you.

intervened? I would've thought more about it. I would have at least tried to catch the woman's eye to see if she deemed herself to be all right.

27 October 2016

There are people worse off than us, he casually understates. This morning I read an article he had suggested in some medical journal about the biology of poverty, about the cortisol levels of babies without structure in their day, whose mothers do not always feed them when they cry. He had read this article over our boiled egg and marmalade on toast with coffee and orange juice, and the infant in his bassinet at our side. After he'd left for work, I planned to read this article as soon as our boy went to sleep. While walking him in a circle and patting his back, swaddled in muslin decorated with fly fishermen, I listened to Fran Kelly interview Missy Higgins about her upcoming Australian tour and the inspiration for her latest album. Missy had given birth to a son shortly before that photograph of a drowned five-year-old asylum seeker was spread across the media. Having a child broke my heart open, she said. I realised then that these raw hormones were ceasing to affect me.

This afternoon he comes home and eats a piece of brownie a friend has baked for us and I ask about his visit to a financial adviser. The adviser offers wealth advisory advice, he says. Wealth advisory advice? I ask. Yes, advice about wealth. As opposed to about tax or business structures. He wants to know how to buy a house before our son starts school. Essentially, the wealth advice is to save money and keep it in the bank. Also, to buy trauma insurance. Trauma insurance will provide a $500,000 lump sum if I get cancer and he has to stop working to care for me. He already has income protection insurance and life insurance. Do any of our friends have trauma insurance? He asks. I shake my head. I'm already the most insured person. Why do I need more insurance? I shrug. I say that a cynic would assume the financial adviser was thinking of their commission. He nods sagely. There are people worse off than us, he says.

Like that Sydney-sider nurse on the *7.30 Report* who believes she and her partner are priced out of the market and will never buy a house. Like the elderly mother and daughter who've moved in together to share rent after two marriage breakdowns and insufficient superannuation. Like the art historian with two small children and a social worker husband, who is renting a property and has only a casual contract at the university. *Life*, I keep typing accidentally, instead of *like*. What a boring, ugly topic to write about, I thought before I started. Who would write about wealth advisers and super. At least I told him off for using *grow* like a politician – grow the economy. Jobs and growth. Boring and ugly it may be, but that is life. Growth.

28 October 2016

Sound has developed
a fibrous quality
I realise at night, trying
to untangle the fine
hair of your sleeping
breath from other noises,
the thunderous crackle
of fresh sheets, your
father's heartbeat.
There it is, I think,
holding my own breath
and hoping. Amazing
how your night sounds
have become so subtle;
how I have the stamina
to lie awake in between

two sleeping bodies,
listening. Yesterday
with your face close
to mine, I inhaled
your exhalation and
it was like pure
oxygen.

29 October 2016

While your father is on the Gold Coast
for a testosterone conference
I have three friends over for dinner and
cards. As we eat chicken salad
and rye bread and drink the cloudy orange
wine Suzie likes, the conversation
runs to dogs (which would you be; how
expensive it is to train a guide
dog). You sit in a small rocking chair
at my feet and gaze up at me
eating, adoring or at least engrossed.
I rock your chair with my left foot
and try not to look at you too often,
try to engage in the discussion,
but your face is as addictive as Facebook;
I say I will quit or limit my views to
a few times a day, yet back I go without
thinking. But there is no guilt;
instead of feeling sickly as though
a decent part of myself is wasting away,
watching you and returning
your expressions seem like the best
way of spending however many hours

of the day. While they list the merits
of Labradors, I remember the elderly
retriever who sat next to your capsule
yesterday morning. The dog was named
Hollywood and she reminded me of Nana,
the canine caretaker of Wendy, John
and Michael in *Peter Pan*. She watched you
as I watch you – with untiring curiosity.

30 October 2016

After our first night alone together,
we have a festive morning listening
to Harry Belafonte and Dusty Springfield
while trying to revive the neglected
herbs on the balcony. You squint
in the sun and I don't worry about
your bare head and feet as the wind
is 25 degrees. I can't recall
the last time you cried. (Yes, I can now;
it was in the pram on the way home
from a birthday party in a park and
you were hungry and I was overly
hot and when we finally wheeled
ourselves into the familiar cool fug
of our hallway and I peeled off
my black jeans and rescued you
from your pram and we stuck
to each other on the sofa and you drank
deeply, stopping only to smile at me;
it was immensely satisfying.)

31 October 2016

All Hallows' Eve,
Melbourne Cup Eve,
US Election Eve Eve.
At the beginning of this
festive week, we wonder
at the number of children
wandering the streets
during school hours. One wears
a black leotard covered only by
a black cape. Her face is behind
a *Scream* mask and in her left hand
she carries a (toy?) knife.
Another has a plastic claw glued
to the end of each finger and a purple
wig. A woman in devil horns tries
to ply a face-painting trade, but
the people who want to be
disguised already are.
We dress as tired parents.
I glimpse my reflection in the op
shop window and the posture
is unfamiliar – my gait is that of
a walker with a frame: craned
forward at the weak waist,
shoulders and spine lazily curved.
Like a made bed with broken
springs, I look subtly wrong –
not obviously flawed, but not
right either. At home, we eat
leftover lamb salad, sardines with
pepper on toast, baba ganoush and
key lime pie with coffee for dessert

(a lunch worthy of an Iris Murdoch
bachelor or Kenneth Grahame's Ratty).[24]
Afterwards, during the baby's playtime,
I lay him on the yoga mat and do
press-ups, bending my elbows to kiss
the baby's forehead before straightening.
It is a dangerous incentive not to collapse.
And, when he is blessedly sleeping again,
I finally begin reading *The Diaries of Miles
Franklin*, which I'd initially overlooked due to
their commencing twenty years after
the period the novel I want to write includes.
The brevity of some entries is inspiring:

24 To Eat

I know this journal is full of food. We are always eating. Eat's Proto-Indo-European origin is not worth mentioning as it is almost identical: *ed*. One of the oldest words, the most human of concerns. When I go back to work I spend my lunch hours pumping milk in the school sickbay. If I forget lunch, or bring something that needs to be heated up and eaten with two hands, I go hungry; doubly hungry. The fat of pregnancy disappears; the fat of my old self goes too. When I remove my winter coat at a friend's birthday drinks, the action accentuates the bones in my chest and her eyes widen. Another friend asks if the balance has tipped – if the baby is eating me alive. It's disingenuous to leave this footnote without admitting that being underweight now exhilarates me in the way that it did when I ate too little and made myself sick when I decided I'd eaten too much during my first year of university. The hall of residence served dinner at 5pm. I usually skipped the queue that snaked past the bain-maries full of deep-fried matter and went straight to the salad bar. If cucumber, beetroot, grated carrot and so forth didn't satisfy me, I would finish with a single slice of wholemeal sandwich bread, smeared with a little margarine and marmalade. Most of my friends were new and did not know my usual diet or dimensions. You can be anyone when you leave home. Disordered eating is typically a Type A personality's mode of controlling her life during periods of change. I don't count myself as a Type A personality; I just wanted to avoid the cliché of what was known at my high school as 'hostel arse' – when you go to uni you get fat. Not me. I went to uni and found my bones wanted to show themselves during literature tutorials. When I first had sex I think I wanted to take up as little of the single hostel bed as possible; to be barely there, physically, seemed attractive. This current lack of weight feels neither attractive nor unattractive. I feel all verb, without time for adjective, yet identifying with several nouns. When Robin says 'Mama', he might mean 'more' or 'mine' or 'milk' or me. I answer every time.

'10 February 1933: Pottered. No peace in house.
No money, hope receding.'[25] Or,
'11 September 1934: Tried to work a little
in spite of maddening conditions and ceaseless
interruptions.' I was going to complain
that this describes my present situation, but
now the house is library-quiet – only four hands
typing on two keyboards, faint traffic
from Heidelberg Road and baby's breath.

1 November 2016

Your father sleeps where he lies
on the floor. You sleep where
you're put, in your bassinet.
I sleep with the couch
cushions imprinting
their texture on my cheek.

When he wakes, your father says
he dreamt about a dangerous water
slide. Perhaps inspired by the tragedy
at Dream World – the seat backs
of wood and rope snapping as if
bitten by a great white shark.

25 To Earn
Plenty of peace, money and hope in the house – just not earned by me. At this time I had zero dollars in my bank account, but was in a position to buy decadent groceries, to use the heater all day, and to get my hair cut thanks to my husband's income. I hadn't been so personally insolvent since I was about fifteen. So lucky to be kept in comfort, but unfortunate to have to be kept. So lucky to not have to leave. So uncomfortable to feel dependent. I still remind myself I am depended upon. There is dignity in being needed and in admitting to need.

When I wake, the last horse is entering
the starting gates of the Melbourne Cup.
I want to boycott the race because
I've decided it is a cruel and tasteless
sport. But – still humming with
chemical sentimentality – I love

the look of the animals in motion and
a story, even one told seven times
in a few minutes. Alamandin's jockey
won the cup sixteen years ago –
the longest a jockey has gone between
wins in this race. What's more, his wife

was due to give birth yesterday and is
the sister of last year's Cup winner.
He seems like a decent man
answering the journalist's awkward
questions as they both trot along
the track – journalist listing to one

side of the saddle as he holds the mic
up to the jockey's quiet mouth. When
the almost-photo-finish is replayed,
I notice that this jockey never uses
his whip – just crouches, light as a cat
trying to hide, over his horse's withers.

2 November 2016

A poet has just visited. She brought soup
and homemade plaited bread and a bib
with colourful owls and a bar of raspberry

soap and advice that there should be no
*should*s, no pushing myself, no obligation
at this vulnerable stage. This vulnerability
will be a strength eventually, she says.
Later, I hurt you for the first time.
It was a ridiculous accident with a toy,
hand-crafted, wooden, painted rainbow
colours in non-toxic paint – a ring to
twist into an infinity sign, with a bell.
As I squatted above you, I dangled
the toy over your giggling face and
somehow dropped it (from what
height?) onto your right eyebrow and
of course you howled. Not quite
the vaccine howl, but enough to
fill my head with glue.
I held you close to my chest and
kissed the eyebrow two hundred times
while walking you around the room
and rubbing your back, repeating
I'm so sorry, between kisses. When
you were quiet but still betrayed,
I fed you from my left breast – the
one that sprays milk at every let
down. When it flooded your mouth,
you pulled away, blinking as it
scattered white freckles over the
red patch on your forehead.
As I stemmed the flow and mopped
your face with a hand towel,
you laughed and I felt absolved.

3 November 2016

It is clear and 22 degrees, so we walk
to Dights Falls and I test the theory
of the poet who visited yesterday –
that this hormonal fug also enables
a special lucidity. What can I see
today that I didn't used to see?
The rainbow edge of the balcony's
glass barrier. The faces painted on
the mugs someone has hung in a
eucalypt next to the Merri Creek.
The autumn leaves decorating
the safety wall alongside the Eastern
Freeway, which we walk beneath,
passing the pigeons' home and the
motivational graffiti: *Even
destruction is a kind of creativity.* The
i's are dotted with hearts. At the Falls
the first thing I notice is three green
rowboats piled on top of each other
at the bottom of the drop. Next,
I see someone has spray-painted
a greeting on the concrete look-out:
Hey Baby! I park your pram next
to the words and take a photo
with the boats in the background.
It is a glorious spring day and
no one else is here. Perhaps it is
an only-child quality of mine,
this pleasure in not having to share
the best weather, except with you.
On the walk back, slightly uphill,
I open my flannel shirt and let

the white nursing singlet and what
it contains reflect the sun. A man
with a dog and a pram who passes
gives a courteous hello and glances
at my breasts, which have never
before warranted such a look.
Now, milk-pale and crazed with
sky blue veins, the still small but
swollen parts curve heavily, making
me feel once again as though I'm in
a borrowed body. These, I think,
are the sort of breasts that could be
treated violently. How does a thought
slip from admiring a pair of lorikeets
feeding on the path to *Titus
Andronicus*-esque acts – slicing off
a breast, for instance and finding
not only blood but a reservoir of
milk. My first reaction to this prospect
is fear for you – what will you eat?
If I'm gone, what will you do?
Is noticing the gore of barely
conscious thoughts the lucidity
the poet mentioned? Or, is it the sense
of meditating as I walk you
in a narrower and narrower circle
around the living room, patting
a heartbeat on your back and listening
to the layers of the world – the ladder
folding up outside the window,
the distant drill, the Harley Davidson
leaving its space across the street,
the voices of smoking businessmen,
birdsong. He is so present, your grandfather

says of you. You require genuine
presence from others too. A perfect
meditation guide, attuned to insincere
attention and asking only that I listen.

4 November 2016

I have not had this dream since
you were born – in fact, I have dreamt
very little in the last three months –

in it I was mother to a baby
that would shrink or disappear
or go missing from my mind –

I was never feeding it enough.
Sometimes it would end up being
a cat. This dream occurs to me now

as you nap downstairs so soundly
that I might forget to be your mother.
But, this brilliant symbiosis we possess

ensures that my front fills up with river
stones if we go too long apart. Early
this morning, 4:30, I woke

to find myself lying on a pile of pebbles
leaking river water and debated with myself
about whether to let you keep sleeping –

whether you needed me as much as I
needed you then. I swear I didn't make a sound,
but a moment after I woke, you yelped

and began sucking your fist,
giving me the signal to carry you
to the front room with the low

light from the lamp, which casts
long shadows of the paper crane
mobile I made. Usually you like

to look at the patterned birds
before drinking, or to look at me.
But, this time, your dreaming mouth

latched on immediately and in ten
minutes of quenching had drained
the river dry and eaten up every stone.

5 November 2016

Remember, remember –
I never can, though – other than
that it is a single-syllable day
in November. There are no
fireworks in Melbourne;
it's a strange thing for New Zealanders
to celebrate anyway. The night is
noisy enough without explosions.
Our friends who visit from Wellington
bring a bib from a gallery in Barcelona,
large and embroidered with a Miró

painting. It would be a good place,
they say, to take a baby – plenty
of things he'd enjoy looking at.
At twelve weeks exactly
he grasps accidentally but firmly
the crackly black-and-white
book of outback creatures,
the wooden ring with the bell,
a clean nappy and surrealism.

6 November 2016

When I was younger I had no qualms
about giving air and light to what now
seems better off private. I feel a fresh
obligation to others whose lives weave
with mine. Before, I suppose, only my own
permission[26] was needed – I rode rough shod
over others' potential embarrassment.

26 To Permit
This manuscript wouldn't exist had I not attended a conference called Poetry and the Essay in December and met Brian Blanchfield, whose essays in his recent book *Proxies* all begin with the incantation: *Permitting Shame, Error, and Guilt, Myself the Single Source.* Brian suggested I read his friend Maggie Nelson's *The Argonauts* in which she mentions the permission other writers attempt to seek from her to write what they most want to and fear to. She cannot confirm the consequences of such exposure, of course, but her example – depicting her family's love in extreme close-up – is galvanising. At this same conference, Jenny Bornholdt read from *The Rocky Shore*, an excerpt about the death of her father, and of her friend Nigel Cox. By the last lines, in which Nigel's five-year-old son is jumping a stile in pursuit of the other children after his dad's ashes have been scattered, I, in the front row, was weeping with involuntary extravagance. In the bathroom after the reading I found other red-eyed writers. During the reading, Jenny invited questions, so I asked about the responsibility of writing about loved ones – Where, I asked, do you draw a line? I don't, she replied, firm and gentle at once. I don't draw a line.

I used to laugh loudly in the room next to
an infant's cot, oblivious to my intrusion.
I used to share secrets with people I thought
would benefit from a portion of someone
else's truth. Now, I empty the dishwasher
like a slow-motion mime, noticing my lack
of depth perception due to a short-sighted
left eye as the lid crashes onto the cast-iron
pot and the pot crashes into the drawer,
and wince at my pollution of the quiet. Now,
I write briefly and discreetly, wondering at
this perverse urge to have others read my words.
When it works, this is poetry, fiction and
autobiography's licence – that the inherent
goodness of promoting fellow feeling and
letting another human know they are not
alone is worth the expense of exposing
private parts of life that are usually
reserved for bathrooms, hospitals and
a select inner circle – lovers, parents.
A.A. Milne's son, Christopher Robin,
complained in adulthood that his father
had climbed upon his infant shoulders,
filched his good name and left him with
the empty fame of being his son.
Recently I read a collection of personal
essays, many of which contained sensitive
portraits of the writer's family. Initially,
the brothers objected to having vignettes
of their lives published, but something
must have changed to make them see
the work as celebratory and loving
rather than exploitative. I used to assume
that if I were the most nakedly flayed

subject of my writing, I could get away
with skinning a few acquaintances too,
but now I see that even if it is just
me on display, there is still a problem:
I no longer own myself.

7 November 2016

The mundane can be hurtful:
my critique of the tightness
of your father's application
of your nappy; my rejection
of his offer to help with bed
time. (He is used to just me –
anything more would be too
stimulating.) I hate having
used the terminology of
parenting self-help books.
Routines can anaesthetise.
What is it about the PhD,
a visiting friend asks, that
lends itself to relationship
breakdowns? I think it is the
lack of shape to each day;
the gaping hole of years
to be filled with your own
investigations about which
few others care. When let
be, free from a nine-to-five
job, one is liable to question
the necessity and value of
other conventions of life –
mealtimes, monogamy.

Routine softens the edges
of your decisions. Without
routine, the decisions become
hazardously sharp. Babies,
according to some books,
crave routine. I keep note
of how each two-hour portion
of the day is spent. Yet
I feel sharp and dangerous.
I can see my own vulnerability
clearly now. At present I rely
on your father; if I were unlucky
enough to need to leave, it would be
difficult. There are reasons beyond
love for keeping the peace.
In the absence of sex, there is
sleep – we fall into it in the same
position every night, with a sort of
superstitious pedantry. However
much we have irritated each other
during the day, there is a space for
my right cheek below his left clavicle;
his left hand cradles my left elbow;
his right hand holds my left.
This is ritual more than routine,
a sort of prayer petitioning for kindness
and forgiveness and honouring
the first times we shared this bed,
long before its navy duvet became
a noisy wave breaking over our killer
whale limbs and threatening to wake
the baby; before the imperatives
of stillness and silence.

8 November 2016

Today, I am reminded of a creature
in one of the Romantic poems I studied
as an undergrad, which metamorphosed
into an array of ghastly forms, and her
lover had to hold on regardless of whether
she was woman, lion, serpent or vampire.
I thought this poem was Keats's *Lamia*,
but the only relevant line I could find was
'she writhed about, convuls'd with silent pain'.
This is what you have turned into since
becoming three months old, though not so
silent. I pace backwards and forwards just
holding, and patting and shushing and hoping
that you will return to your gentle two-month-
old temperament, or, at least, to sleep and
wake to feed[27] as you used to, with gusto,
focussing on the task instead of arching
your strong spine, twisting your mouth and bellowing.
Yes, my shape-shifter, the glass bottle and BPA-free
teat are becoming necessities as of tomorrow,
when, somehow, a version of myself must leave you
for several hours and interview for a job
teaching English and philosophy to teenagers,
who shape-shift too, in their own way. I must
take on a more ironed surface,
try to look less like an unseaworthy vessel,
not fit for any serious journey.

27 To Wake
I can't reread this line without hearing the first stanza of Theodore Roethke's villanelle 'The Waking': 'I wake to sleep, and take my waking slow. / I feel my fate in what I cannot fear. / I learn by going where I have to go.' Those full-stops, a deliberate lack of enjambment, suggest a baulking at the inevitable, the fated: I like it very much.

9 November 2016

Early on the morning of my job interview
I walk you into the wardrobe. Our multiple skins
hanging, uncanny as a portal to another
world in a strange, comfortable darkness.
You relax, unaware of our impending parting.

Driving along Exhibition Street, bisecting
the CBD, one can appear to function
normally after a combined total of three hours'
sleep. Props (sunglasses, car keys,
a drapy jacket and black-and-white leather
shoes) can make one look employable.

When I arrive, the school smells familiar. This
surprises me; I was only there a few months.
It's all grass clippings and roses outside,
sweet wood polish and wool inside.
My shoes clop a reassuring beat on the foyer
floor and the portraits of former principals

gaze benevolently (if not actually smiling)
at me. I do not miss him at present.
I like walking bipedal and straight-backed
without a pram in front or a capsule balanced
like a heavy picnic basket over my arm or
a carrier strapped on, or even a pregnant girth.

Unencumbered, even by old anxieties and nerves,
I perform well in the interview. It's easier to speak
of my former achievements this time, as it feels
as though I'm talking about someone else, distant
and foreign and faintly glamorous for it. Oh, yes,
I think, she – that capable person – can do this.

10 November 2016

Was it the sound of the bathwater
being thrown out? Nobody likes
to get out of a warm bath, but
this response was disproportionate.
It helps to read about synaptic
development, your cortisol levels and
sensitivities that lead to such red-
faced screams, delicate features
squeezed into an unrecognisable
shape. Is it because we were needling
each other as we dressed you? I don't
like the way you do that, when he
tugged the singlet over your face,
squashing your nose. Was the quick kiss
too startling – did my giant witch's nose
bump your beautiful miniature version?
You will never remember this unless
it is stored subconsciously, but I cried too
as you vomited into the space between us,
gluing your Wondersuit to my sweatshirt,
as your father ran you another warm bath,
stripped you with medical efficiency and
dipped you back in the water, all the while
your screams choking you and your face puce.
It was not until, still warm, naked and almost
dry, you lay against my own bare chest with
a white towel over your back and I squirted
milk into your howling mouth, you began
to calm. It is possible to drink and scream,
you proved, but gradually the sweet lactose
worked its magic and your face returned
to a familiar shape. Your eyes lost their flat,

possessed texture and shined into mine.
Is it possible that you were speaking for us?
Loud little oracle, lamenting the new president.

11 November 2016

I lie on my stomach to identify
the muscles and technique
I'd use to roll onto my back.
I lie on my stomach to show you
how the elbows can become
a support – that the back and neck
need not do all the work of holding
the head high. I lie on my stomach
and remember the months when
this posture was impossible.
I lie on my stomach to stop
the dormant biceps and abdominals
from withering. I lie on my stomach
and see dust gathering under the coffee
table, explaining your sneezes. I lie
on my stomach and watch your face.
I could watch your face all day, I say.

12 November 2016

In a suit covered with kind fluorescent tigers
he holds a knitted zebra with a bell in its stomach.
He brings the zebra's ear to his mouth, and then its hoof.
He holds it by the tail and swings the creature, experimental,
listening to the rattle. He dangles the creature and drops it,
watching me watching. Our carnivore's fat fingers
with dimpled knuckles are finally dextrous.

12 November 2016

As you learn how to swing a zebra by the tail
and to hold your rabbit's paw while
you sleep, your other behaviours are changing
too. I no longer know when you are hungry
and you seem incensed when offered
the breast a moment too early or
too late. You are understandably
exhausted and this state has given you
a horror of sleeping. Suddenly, you realise
how uncomfortable your life is
the moments of cold after the warm
bath, the tug of a garment over your head,
the snag of a fingernail. You are an acute
observer of discomforts and seem
to associate them all with me.

4

13 November 2016

The lens adjusted and the view cleared
when I watched a youngish man, athletic build,
turn and stare at a man of similar age
walking with a twisted gait, pigeon-footed,
his left arm a stiff hook. He had dropped his
phone, but managed to loop his plastic shopping
bag handle over his bent wrist and use
his dextrous hand to retrieve his phone.
As he passed me, he gave me the smile
of someone accustomed to being stared at,
at having to expend more energy on
small tasks. I smiled back, automatic, although
wet around the eyes under my sunglasses.
And, then I noticed the man in front of me turn
to stare, and the view, as I said, cleared.
Without seeing his eyes, hidden behind
wrap-around sunglasses, it was an ambiguous
double-take, but the way he sucked his cigarette,
his own easy gait, and his buzz-cut blond hair,
and rugby shorts, all signalled to me
that his initial reaction to this man was disgust.
That says more about me, of course; he could just as
easily have been thinking, Should I have helped?
And feeling pity. Just because he looked like
a Trump voter or a One Nation supporter
does not mean that he is one. It was this analysis
that distracted me from what I must look like –
a nobody (no pregnant stomach, no pram)
wearing too little for the cold weather but feeling
only my tear-hot face, unable to mind
the numbing wind, carrying the umbrella
weakly, unlikely to bother using it if the next

shower came before I got home. Home,
which I'd been invited to leave. Why don't you go
for a walk, he instructed, holding you, as we both
sobbed. Home, where I'd made my first serious error
with you, and which until that clarifying moment
I did not know how to return to.

Never cry in front of your child. A GP friend
with three children gave this advice once and
I wondered what such restraint would do
to a mother. My own sobbing was a surprise.
During the previous hours of trying to settle
you to sleep, I see now that I was gradually
unhinging. I'd tied a piece of string to the stem
of the bird of paradise leaf that you enjoy staring at
so that I could jiggle it while chopping vegetables
for dinner, a small distance from you. And then,
I pushed your bassinet too fast, so the wheels
would be heard downstairs and sound angry.
They were not heard, I don't think, but you
recognised the anger and your expression
changed. Guilty, I picked you up and cuddled you
again, then sat on the couch, exhausted from walking
in circles. I thought about feeding you, but did not
feel ready to cope if you refused to drink yet again,
kicking and scratching at my chest. So I lay you
on my knee as I do when we pull silly faces
at each other and you learn to laugh, but instead
of playing, I – without meaning to – started to cry.
And you, your face tensed as if I had dropped
a wooden toy on your forehead, as if I had inflicted
pain, and you began to sob too. What's the matter?
Finally, he came. He came up the stairs and took you
and I told him I could not get you to sleep

and he told me to go for a walk to the shop
to buy us an ice cream, and I tried to leave
immediately, but had difficulty moving, difficulty
imagining where I would go and how I would talk
to a stranger. In the corner store – the first place
I visited when home from hospital, the first place
I took you in your pram – I kept my sunglasses on
and said as little as possible.

14 November 2016

Today we miss parents' group
so that you can sleep, and you do
sleep for three hours. The house is
strangely quiet; outside strangely
loud (why must the sliding door
of your white van be slammed, why
must you set your smoke alarm
off every day, why the footsteps,
the key in the lock). I know it is
important to leave the house, for
sanity, so as soon as you wake and
feed, we will take our usual trip
to the vegetable shop, and we will
smell the roses and honeysuckle
and feel the unseasonable breeze
and be glad to live in a city that
doesn't traverse a faultline and
be glad to have each other.

*

Remember the things you've done
well. Remember listening to his cry

and holding vainly to his twisting
muslin body and thinking, why
keep walking when it is clearly not
pleasing him. Remember putting him
gently on the bed and lying down too
and how his face changed. You can't
lie to a baby. That is why he was so
strange with me when I returned
from yesterday's desperate walk.
He did not know what to make of
this trembling clown's face of a
smile. When you lay on the bed and
looked at him closely, he knew
you were not merely walking and
thumping his behind in a steady
hypnotic rhythm, but trying
to communicate as he is trying.
Remember how he likes to talk
to you last thing at night as he
feeds. In between mouthfuls he
licks his lips and stares you in the
eye and solemnly says, Ah-ah-ahh.
And you reply with equal solemnity,
because laughing now confuses him.
He is straining to tell you what
you may already know or what you're
yet to grasp. You think of an alien
asking to be taken to a leader.

15 November 2016

Again pacing, again singing,
this time holding my phone

out of your sight and reading
the late Leonard Cohen's lyrics
and finding them most appropriate.
You join in with your *ah-ah-ahhs*
at the chorus and it sounds
more like 'Hallelujah' than my own
wobbling melody. After realising
you are hungry, I sit on the bed
and feed you and play Jeff Buckley's
version so that you know what
singing should sound like.
You pull off the breast as if
startled by an epiphany when
you hear his voice and I tell you,
yes, that is the right reaction.

16 November 2016

I am making you a book for Christmas.
Its flaws are metaphors for the qualities
you may inherit from me rather than
from your father – the rough-cut pages,
poorly measured, the many layers
of paper and card hiding mistakes, the
shine of spilt PVA glue, wiped off
messily, the unravelling thread holding
the pages together, the cock-eyed drawings
of birds. But, it will be finished in time,
I vow to myself, imperfect as it is,
it will exist and it will be just for you.

17 November 2016

Whoever said the definition of insanity is doing
the same thing multiple times even when it
doesn't work has not had the task of making
an infant sleep. Pacing and patting and singing
and swinging and shushing repeatedly, I knew
it was impossible to do the same thing twice
for each action changes according to the context,
like the subtle light and shadow across the baby's
face as I walk back and forth beside the stairs
and watch the eyelids lower, flicker, close and
switch open again. I can hold him the same way
so many times that I find and ruin new muscles
in my neck, back and arms, yet he responds
differently repeatedly. I shush so much that I
shush my husband and myself. When the bones
in my ankle cracked as I tried to creep away
from the cot, I shushed, as the door brushed
the corner of the duvet, I shushed. I do the same
things day after day and find myself becoming
a different person.

18 November 2016

The baby likes the face of a friend who visits
and her long dark hair that fits well in his fist
and her big, kind smile that mirrors his silly
grin. Perhaps he likes her slight incense-like
smell that resembles his lavender and camomile
baby oil. Perhaps he knows she is a social worker
and good at talking to anyone. When he is sick
of being walked about by me, he sits happily

in this new lap and laughs – a breathy,
ridiculous *ha ha ha* – at this new friend's face.

19 November 2016

We fight over a small white towel.
You take one upstairs
and I say, I already have a white towel
upstairs. I must be deaf to my tone,
because you say I snapped – Why be so
angry over a small white towel?
Neither of us is. I think we are angry
because both of us have been very
good this morning – you have done
the washing and I have made breakfast.
The boy is fast asleep at the right
hour. We are so pleased with our own
contributions that we fail to notice
the work of the other. A small white
towel resembles the flag flown
by warships declaring a truce.
After a shower, I still lack the words
for an honest apology, but instead
I kiss your head and you touch
my arm. We both douse
the baby in affection.

20 November 2016

On the Facebook page for parents
in the Darebin area, someone asks
about primary schools. Fairfield is

good, according to several members,
but not especially multicultural.
Walking to the Fairfield shops today,
we pass white picket fences and white
roses and white lapdogs and white-
haired homeowners. In the newspaper
this morning I read about a white
journalist fired for a racially abusive
tweet about Michelle Obama. The nine-
year-old son of an acquaintance said
that he couldn't marry his best friend,
not because his best friend is a boy too,
but because he is Vietnamese. This boy
goes to a 'multicultural' school, but
doesn't know any mixed-race couples
so he assumed it wasn't allowed.

21 November 2016

Nearly 40 degrees today and all the hot babies
at parents' group had their fat thighs showing.
All those creases in legs and arms, around wrists
and ankles – dimples where knuckles and elbows
will be. Eczema flaring and cheeks like Pacific Rose
apples and cradle cap cracking like yellow sand.
Robin held his friend Owen's hand again and
the two three-month-old boys stared back
over their heads into the blind-dimmed light
of the window, transfixed by the same nothing,
suggesting that there is an acute sense of
sight that perhaps we outgrow; their mothers
had eyes only for those soft fingers entwined.

22 November 2016

It isn't the ache in the lower back caused by the peculiar
hips-forward, muscle-less posture the physio told you
to avoid, or, really, the senselessness of pacing the same
track around the bedroom (between bed and cot towards
the lamp; other side of bed past his shoes; into the dark
of the wardrobe; into the light of the en suite, touch the back
door; repeat) but the fear of torturing the baby with boredom.
You suspect he needs to sleep, you know he does not want to;
you realise the methods of soothing, if performed with increased
force, become forms of abuse – the patting of the nappied bottom
could turn into smacking, the swinging into shaking, the shushing
into a whispered yell. You hold all these possibilities
inside as firmly as you hold the boy, having to readjust your grip
as often as you lie him on the bed to wrap escaped limbs back into
the swaddle. You consider the many ways that you have failed
in this task: too long, wrong track, clumsy transition from carrying
to cot, too impatient. The other evening at the Edinburgh Gardens
in 30-degree heat you watched the baby relax and fall asleep
in a friend's arms. This friend, you know, loves small children.
He was relishing holding your one, holding him as if he could happily
do so forever, admiring the miniature nose and fat, pre-pedal feet.
This is what must be achieved, I know, a convincing love of the
moment, however long it lasts, before he sleeps. The infinity sign
shape that you swing him in must appear to endure all restlessness,
every back arch and wail. You must persuade him this carrying is
unconditional and permanent – never-ending. And then he will sleep.

23 November 2016

It is a very messy business, being god
of a new world. Instead of teaching

through play, I mop up the milky way –
curds and whey splashing over the duvet
and floorboards, wetting the dust collecting
under the bed. While I mop, the world
lies in his cot and enjoys his mobile –
the fluffy vehicles turning in time to
Go to sleep, little baby. It makes no sense
to spend hours waiting for the world's
eyes to close – but a good god knows
that every world needs sleep if it is to grow.

24 November 2016

Listening to the radio and wondering
whether it should be turned off in order
to help him fall asleep, I hear an American
academic's lecture on the role of care[28] in
Western society. She tells an anecdote
about receiving surgery: the nurse
apologised for leaving her just before
going to theatre, as she had to collect

---

28 To Care

From the Old Norse *kor* for 'sickbed', care's origins emphasise grief and lament rather than changing sheets and feeding. Caring is traditionally women's work; the caring professions of nursing and teaching feminine and underpaid. 'Why do you spend so much on a nanny when there are cheaper options like an au pair?' a young colleague asks. I say it seems wrong to begrudge the person looking after my most important thing in the world a proper wage and working conditions. If I am complicit in diminishing the significance of care, then how can I complain about the paucity of maternity leave, of the sense that I am freeloading off my husband while staying at home with our son when he goes to work. Once, when I mentioned a friend's financial situation to my father, he explained it by saying she'd have access to her father's credit card. Parents', I corrected. Father's, he said again, oblivious. Parents', I repeated. Parents', then, if you like, he said, tone deformed (I hope) by my bitter memory into complete condescension.

her children from school. The care
this nurse provides should be viewed
as equally important as the surgeon's
role, regardless of the respective years
of study each person undertook, the relative
'skill'. I realise, as the academic's voice
muffles behind the closed bedroom door,
as my socks slide over the familiar path
and my lower back takes on its usual throb,
that I am resisting the role of carer as
the baby is resisting sleep. He is whimpering,
afraid of being alone, perhaps, or bored
by the repetitive turns around the room,
deeply in need of the rest, but fighting it.
My job is to rub and pat and swing him
into the frightening dullness of rest, and
I am resisting it when I glance at my watch
and pine for what I have been conditioned
to deem more important – the finishing
of the novel about women trying to balance
care and competitiveness; the studying
of literacy and preparation for work;
the calling of the nanny agencies – arranging
someone else to fulfil this necessary
role of ensuring the baby is healthy, happy,
sleeping, eating, growing. Patti Smith
gets annoyed when journalists ask about
her long hiatus between albums. What
did she do with those years? She raised
a son and a daughter. What else?

25 November 2016

We are sleeping together. We sleep
together all night long – eight hours
in a row. I am sure a stand-up comedian
has made this joke; but, it's true:
sleep replaces sex. How much
are you getting, the mothers
at the new parents' group ask,
taking care not to reveal smugness
or envy. It is fetishised, this human
need. Say the word a hundred times
and it dissolves like the gluey tears
I wipe with a cotton ball from the baby's
lashes. The meaning slips. What is
a good sleep? Last night, after a day
of arched-back screaming when offered
milk, and cooing sadly when walked back
and forth towards his cot, the boy slept eight
and a half hours straight and I woke with
middens on my chest. Except, instead
of refuse, these piles of shells and stones
and bones could be massaged into sustenance.[29]

29 To Wean
From Old English *wenian* meaning 'to accustom, habituate', it is not primarily the baby
who needs to learn to desire a new routine, but me. The concept of maternal finitude, which
Maggie Nelson discusses in *The Argonauts*, is familiar. The milk is finite; what I as a mother
can provide is finite. My current bounteous, milkful identity is temporary. When it ends, I
will need to find another way to be or feel as crucial to my son. Or, I will need to admit to
myself that every minute I am less relevant, and that this diminishment of my necessity to his
existence will continue until my death. Perhaps that is why I struggle to stop feeding him, and
write so much about the act; it bolsters my ego. Also, I hate to say no to him, when what he
requests is so nourishing. Also, I am still surprised that the small breasts I've never really liked
much have performed their purpose so well.

I lifted the boy from his cot before
he had time to wake and feel the stress
of hunger, and he drank prodigiously,
instinctively, without opening
his eyes or kicking his legs, just a subtle
twitch of the feet, keeping time
with the rhythm of the milk.
You know it is a proper sleep when
there is time for a nightmare.
I do not remember what panicked me,
just him nudging my back and saying,
Amy, wake up. Wake up. I wouldn't.
I was lost in the plot, whatever it was,
clinging on simply because it was sleep.

26 November 2016

Journals are more often letters of complaint than celebration;
when the day is so easy that you go to an artists' market in the garden
of a gallery, carrying the baby on your front and holding his tiny
socked feet in each hand as you walk past stalls selling crocheted
cat collars, handmade soaps flavoured with lemon myrtle and leather
bags embossed with fantails, there is little need to write. Instead,
you notice that you and perhaps other market-goers are performing
their relaxation. Yes, the dog roses are picturesque and a gentle
undulation of screen-green grass grazed by yellow and red
corrugated-iron cows is whimsical, but how many bird bags
does a person need? You blessedly slept as I drove up and down
the hill for thirty-five minutes looking for a car park, before parking half
a kilometre past the Heidelberg Country Club (with its own vast,
empty car park and a small sign saying *All unauthorised vehicles
will be towed*). For every stall of artisanal jewellery, textiles and prints,
there must have been fifteen cars. Holding your feet and kissing

your cradle-capped head repeatedly as we circled past the speaker playing folk music, the organic beer stall and the espresso cart, I felt like a tourist.

27 November 2016

We walk to the playground next to the Merri Creek to meet a friend and her twins with assonant names. She compares your flaking cradle cap to a prehistoric egg hatching a dinosaur. She encourages her daughter to kiss you on the hand. You watch the older children swinging and fail to laugh, a serious expression broken only by sneezes. Neither of us wears the right number or type of layers in this spring of thunderstorm asthma, minute particles of pollen, thirty-eight degrees followed by ten, rain, sun and gales. I worry you are about to stop breathing or burn whenever we leave the safety of the house. I am privately delighted when I see a lump of snot, apple green and the circumference of your nostril sitting on your upper lip. I flick it into the grass and quietly congratulate you, as I do every time you lose a bit of extraneous matter.

28 November 2016

It is time to begin thinking
about English and philosophy –
apparently I will be teaching three
Year 12 subjects. It is time to consider that
teaching means lives other than my son's
are my responsibility. It is time to remember
what it is like to have six three-hour exams
thundering towards you, hooves drumming
inevitably louder as the year progresses.
While the baby catches his first viruses,
cuts his first teeth, says his first words and
takes his first steps, seventy-five teenagers

will be practising writing essays, memorising
definitions, interpreting texts. And I, I must
put aside any half-written novels and struggle,
vicarious, with other people's milestones.

29 November 2016

Like Tinder, I guess – finda
babysitter.com. She's my age,
has studied English lit and classics,
gave birth the same month I did.
In references from other parents,
she resembles Mary Poppins.
I begin imagining life with her.
She will be more than a nanny –
our sons will be friends. My phone
stays near me at all times and
I check my email for a response
(she is a 'quick responder').
We seem alike, so I like her.
I hope that you will like her too.
Perhaps it's more akin to Tindering
on someone else's behalf, for an
amicable ex, say; I'm looking
for someone you will like, but not
more than you like me. She will smell
of milk too. In a fantasy I am hospitalised
after a car accident or similar and
there is not enough expressed milk
in the freezer, so she feeds you her own.
This dream becomes a nightmare
when I sleep. She does not feature
literally, but I am stuck at work – not

school, the uni, except it is a pub and
my students are drunk, and I am covering
for a lecturer whose emails are all broken
lines and faux rebellion when really
he is insulated by job security and has
forgotten how unethical his employer is.
I have forgotten my glasses and can't read
his notes and know that it is four hours
since you have been fed and I do not know
where you are. In this dream I meet
the guitarist from my ex's band and he is
emaciated, bleeding from a head wound
and muttering about adding to his family.
When I wake to your sleeping
grizzle and slurp of the fist at 2:20am
it is a relief like water down my always
dehydrated throat to take you
to the low-lit feeding room and feed.

30 November 2016

On the to-do list today
was drawing a pardalote,
possibly vacuuming, going
to the irritating organic
supermarket and buying
curry paste, arranging
a meeting with the dream
nanny and writing –
writing anything, really.
This morning I read
an interview with an old
acquaintance whose novel

will soon be a television series,
of which she is the executive
producer and screenwriter.
None of the dialogue
could be lifted from the novel;
it all had to be rewritten
for the purposes of suspense.
The plot had to be reordered
to appeal to the audience.
I feel, reading this, the usual
schadenfreude and pride
and wistfulness and spur
to do something important
and successful immediately.
Then the boy wakes and I
hold his weight and admire
his healthy complexion and
realise quicker than usual how
vain and ungrateful I am to wish
myself the creator of anything
other than what I have made.
The novel I would dearly like
to have written but refuse to write
haunts me like a cliché. I fear
its historical inaccuracies
and poor sentences, so neglect it
like friends I'm too ashamed to call
because it has been so long.

1 December 2016

To write while the baby is awake is cheating.
He, like most, is yet to see this as work –
prefers watching me fold
washing or dry dishes or cook dinners,
unless he is allowed to look at the black letters
scurrying across the screen.
Now, he is lying in his forest with a red-faced lion
under his left arm and a squirrel dangling
above the fingers of his right hand.
He fills the mat with his kicks and flails as if
growing deliberately before my eyes.
We have given back the plastic teal baby
bath and bags of quadruple-zero clothes and
the white bassinet. Soon, we will pass on
this playmat to a new baby and move
ours into a larger habitat than the Garden
of Eden / Snow White's Wood
rattling with plush flora and fauna.
An apple with a mirror glued to its back
flashes light across his face. He loves his own
reflection without knowing what it is,
but sometimes is overwhelmed and has to
bury his face in my clavicle, escaping
the awful significance of himself.

2 December 2016

I have a detailed inventory to help me
with cramming all the boy's paraphernalia
into the zippable side of my suitcase,
so, instead of packing I take him to his first

film, assuming that 11am at the Palace
Westgarth on a clear, 26-degree day,
when a biopic about the founder of McDonald's
is playing, will be cool and empty.
I arrive late and find the aisles gridlocked
with strollers. The infants are surprisingly
quiet, jowls lit by the screen, gummy
mouths open, staring at Michael Keaton's
giant ambitions not for revolutionising
the food industry but for making money
and revolting disdain for his wife's lack
of entrepreneurial spirit. It is the flat,
soggy version of the American Dream
rather than the pack shot of the towering
construction of multiple patties, pickles,
mustard and buns. The baby enjoys
watching the parents in the row behind us,
over my shoulder. He is dumbfounded
by the 1950s panorama and occasionally
startled by the slamming of a car door or
yell from the once-milkshake salesman.
When he is tired, he requires me to stand
at the edge of the cinema and sway with him
close to my chest and a palm over his exposed
ear, like other mothers. When he sleeps,
I lie him along my thighs and watch the film.
Briefly, it is almost as though he doesn't exist.

3 December 2016

I am aware of my ears and eyes
of the altitude and the light
as I haven't been in years,

for I am divided – part large
and old, part new and small;
when he squints and winces,
I feel it in multiple ways at once,
confusing as a Cubist portrait,
strangely familiar and moving,
moving fast along the runway,
juddering – his eyes and mine
holding each other's gaze
as my arm holds his body and
his hand holds the edge of my
singlet and his mouth holds my
nipple and the milk holds the
sides of his throat as he sucks
not just for sustenance but
apparently knowing what
the swallowing can do.

4 December 2016

My dear friend and her Huntaway
give up their bedroom for the night
we stay in Wellington. She warns us
not to put the portacot under the tall
bookcase; in the last quake, everything
fell off – Davis, Hemingway,
Borges, Solnit. We don't want
you to get buried in short stories and
memoir. This friend has a room
of her own where she writes screenplays.
There is a vintage picture of a growling
panther to the left of the desk
and fluorescent letters Blu-Tacked above

and below the cat's face saying, WORK
HARDER. 'I can make one for you,' my friend
says, when I tell her about the neglected novel,
which I am considering turning into a novella
or collection of poems, not because that is the best
form for the idea but due to lack of time or
more likely courage. Fear makes my lines brittle.
In case a novella is the right form, my dear
friend lends me Roberto Bolaño's *A Little
Lumpen Novelita* to read in Hawke's Bay or
at the airport or whenever the time allows.
By the end of the first page I feel refreshed
by the – even in translation – diamond-sharp
voice. My dear friend's dog has a vocabulary
of three hundred words; she barks when
I say 'cat' and knows which soft toy to fetch
when my friend says 'monkey' or 'koala'.
The filmmaker and dog live in a house
they own within the tsunami red zone.
There are symbols everywhere. For that salty
air and cold wind and view of the ferry
beginning to cross the Cook Strait, one risks
being drowned. I frequently use the fault line
as an excuse for not moving home; too
dangerous; it is nice to live in a stable
city – the only threats are fires and
terrorist attacks. I have a recurring dream
in which I am sitting in an unfamiliar car
and confusing the accelerator, break and
clutch. 'What could it mean?' I ask you,
knowing that you don't believe dreams
mean anything. Now I realise the clutch
is my favourite of the pedals – a means of
changing without committing to stopping

or starting. When learning to drive
my instructor would scold me for 'coasting'
downhill, pressing the clutch and relieving
myself of the need to choose a gear.

5 December 2016

This is written later –
being at home relieved me of the need
to turn the journey into words. Just
interpreting the familiar smells and
showing my son the benevolent
head of the elderly horse in the front
paddock, letting him break the surface
of the swimming pool with his fat warm
feet, giving him smears of avocado off
my index finger and holding his nose
above citrusy sprays of star jasmine.
At the beach where my mother
tells me, in an unusual text message,
I was conceived, it is too bright
for young eyes so he sleeps with his face
pressed into my supersternal notch,
a bucket hat covered in big game fish –
a gift from his grandparents – shading
the back of his neck. I walk through
shin-deep waves and hope he hears the sea.

6 December 2016

The architecture of a woman's brain
changes, according to recent research,
during pregnancy and in the two years
after having a baby. We visit my school
friend and sit on her deck in the sun,
admiring the roses, the lawn, the fruit
trees and treehouse, the trampoline and
the white-haired three-year-old boy
whose expressions are oddly identical
to those of my fourth-form maths teacher (her dad),
and the solemn-eyed daughter with damp
curls who wants to be complimented
on her dress. The three have made
an orange and sultana cake. My friend's
husband says she is amazing, always
having fresh baking on the table, despite
two kiddies and a third on the way.
I knew she was amazing when we were fourteen,
writing Victorian love letters to each other
on the whiteboard during rainy lunchtimes and
perplexing our classmates, who probably
presumed we were lesbians. She was a jazz singer
and pianist, and wanted to be an investigative journalist.
I think she is amazing now, rolling her eyes
at her husband's suggestion of sending their eldest
to boarding school provided he doesn't turn out to be
a 'softer soul'. The hippocampus shrinks to make
room for a lobe that lets the mother interpret
her baby's thoughts almost telepathically. I find
my long-term memory is sharper – that parts
of myself I have missed are returning, confusingly
introducing themselves to new versions.

7 December 2016

Around the outdoor table on the back lawn
we drink coffee from mugs with orange
blossom or sheepdogs on the side and eat
Dad's date scones, with a little cinnamon,
and Mum's lemon and coconut cake and
the parents of my oldest friends arrive,
looking hungrily at the baby. It is difficult
to talk about anything other than him,
although their son is soon to be married
and their daughter has just completed
a degree in counselling and one of them
has survived leukaemia and the other
works as a nurse and neither of them
has met my husband before. But
mainly we discuss whether the sun
is in the baby's eyes and what his red
expression might mean and if that was
really a smile. When we crunch across
the lime-sand drive to wave goodbye
to their car, the one whose gifts are always
too generous pulls a ring off her finger and
says: I didn't want to make a fuss. It's for me,
she says, because it's an opal, the stone
for October babies (we share a birthday)
and she doesn't want to wait until
a special occasion or until she is dead
and my friend has other items
in her inheritance and won't notice,
or at least won't mind, if I am wearing
her mother's old opal ring. It fits over
my large knuckle. I can only thank her.

8 December 2016

A friend warned me months ago
that my baby would start to smell
of other people – perfumes, creams,
colognes, sweat – your baby's head
will press against strangers' throats
and décolletage, held close and warm.
Sure enough I recognised the musky,
woody scent of our family friend in his hair
and skin yesterday long after she'd left.
Babies are olfactory creatures, happiest
emanating their own or their parents'
odour. We squirt Johnson's shampoo
under the running tap for the mānuka
sweetness it leaves behind his ears.
Now, he is strapped against me and
I am afraid the sunscreen on my chest
will distract from the baked tussock,
sandy fragrance fresh and familiar
as a wave,[30] blue and white as the baby's
eyes. We walk along Ocean Beach towards

---

30 To Wave
To move to and fro, from the Old Norse *vagr* meaning billowing water. Waves, Robin, look!
We squinted into the glare of the mid-morning horizon as we paddled along the edge of the
Bass Strait. His right hand lifted and twisted back and forth, to and fro at the breakers.

I am wavering between then and now. This is our third time at Skene's Creek. The first
was the first weekend away with my partner – my first conventional weekend away with any
partner. He booked a cabin whose view from the bedroom window was dense and private
with eucalypts and which was all sea and sky from the balcony, where I sat typing away at my
thesis with a beer while he barbecued us fresh fish. I had about $36 in my bank account and
was both luxuriating in and anxious about the incongruity of this experience. In the spa bath
we sucked each other's toes and played with the jets. The photos I took were all of us – our feet
the same size and sandy, only distinguishable by my red nail polish and bandaged toe; him on
the swing, a joyful blur of beard and beer.

Cape Kidnappers, which is only ever a haze
of coast in the distance, past macrocarpas,
painted black in the Dick Frizzell print
on my parents' bedroom wall. We walk and
the baby's sleeping cheek sticks to my skin.

9 December 2016

There are creases in the back
of my father's tanned neck, like
Hemingway's old man. He spends
two hours longer than usual out
in his boat, trying to catch enough
kahawai for our dinner. It is filleted,

The second time we came to this beach we stayed at the same cabin, but the weather was miserable. I photographed the food we made and the special bottle of wine we drank and my partner's back as he walked away from me in his red jacket along the deserted beach. We brought our yoga mats and held postures together while rain hung white in the trees, obscuring the sea. I had just got my period for the twelfth time of hoping it wouldn't come and was allowing myself to drink the wine, which tasted of nothing. We still didn't know why I wasn't getting pregnant, or how to fix it, or how lucky we would be when the weeks of injections started.

This time we are staying in a family's beach house. I move the bowls of shells and driftwood ornaments to higher ground. My partner blocks the steps from the deck to the wild garden with three chairs. We coax our toddler not to use the length of timber dowel locking the sliding door in place to drum on the glass coffee table. We find empty snail shells, stones of all varieties and point at the sulphur underside of the wings of the cockatoos, which shriek en masse as they fly. I photograph the baby in the hammock, the baby in the sea, the baby scooping sand into his bucket; his face is always behind a broad-brimmed sunhat patterned with leaves. After seven, when Robin is asleep, we play quiet games of Scrabble and Monopoly at the outdoor table, drinking wine and eating chocolate to keep warm. On every visit I've forgotten how cold the beach gets at night and pack inadequately. This time I bring socks but no shoes, and many T-shirts but no heavy jersey. Like an eighteen-month-old I wear socks and sandals and eccentric layers. To warm up after swimming in the sea, we all shower together. I show Robin how I wash my face by closing my eyes and dipping my head under the stream. My partner demonstrates how he washes his face, carefully with a flannel. We both applaud when Robin's wet eyelashes open and he smiles.

barbecued and served with a Persian
marinade from a cookbook I gave
my mother two Christmases ago.
The recipe calls for dried rose petals.
She picks them from her own garden
and lays them out in the sun (and
later microwaves, to speed the process).
She lets the baby take handfuls
of petals off the ageing bunch in
the dining room. He scatters them
romantically across the floorboards.
Later, I find one still clutched, bruised,
perfumed and bright as blood in his fist.

10 December 2016

I don't want to go and have not admitted it
for many years. As we turn left out of the gate
between the beech trees which have grown
vastly more than me in the last thirty years
I weep, at first secretive and then in such a way
that demands a question from you. You always
ask even if the reason seems obvious to me,
for the reason is seldom logical and you find
logic the highest necessity, reminding me
of the structures of the world that won't budge
despite my wishes and offering to find a way
to help me around or over or to accept that
there is no way out that isn't violent and
unorthodox. Why are you upset? you ask
eventually. Because, it will never get any
easier, I say – by the time I try to explain
the reason has always engorged to a lumpy

shape and the words are blocked. What
won't get easier? you ask. The leaving,
the guilt, the wanting to stay but also not
wanting to. Coddling these reasons is
a watery substance – the impending
separation from the baby. Today, my idea of
paradise is staying in Hawke's Bay and
spending my days writing and caring
for my child. But, of course, if this wish
were granted it would be at the expense
of Melbourne, employment and you. I am
often reminded of what a veteran New Zealand
expatriate poet in Melbourne told me years ago,
when my life was very different: You think
there are choices, but really there is only one.

11 December 2016

We cross the Remutaka Range under sheets
of rain and I remind him to be cautious
of the corners pointing to the faint white
of the road ahead twisting and rising
like smoke. Just over the summit
a motorcyclist in front of us slips off,
the machine skidding on its side,
the rider's left leg underneath for
less than a minute as we stop and
watch, will the leather limbs to
gather themselves and stiffly wheel
the bike to the narrow edge. The rider's
friend passes us and pulls over. We continue,
wipers slicing the water from left to right
and back again and I think of how wet it must be

on the side of the road, having the whole
slippery range to ride down with one bad leg.
When we are most distracted by the conditions –
afraid of something larger than sleep or milk –
the baby is quiet, either lulled by the rain
or sensing his parents' relief from himself.

12 December 2016

We arrive in customary Wellington weather,
thick reams of horizontal rain, fast and sharp
as a brand new printer spitting out pages
of a novel not ready to be read – reminding me
of the machine monitoring contractions almost
exactly four months ago. We arrive at a hotel
we can't afford, where there is art –
a taxidermied piglet in make-up –
for the baby to examine while I check in.
Our room is large, dark, quiet and its windows
overlook the lap pool. I pad across the gold
and plum fleur de lis carpet away from
the portacot containing a person whose head
flicks violently side to side as he falls asleep
as if consciousness is a fly irritating his eyes.
When he stills, we both relax into our books.
Eventually, as his breath evens out into miniature snores,
we are brave enough to whisper to each other
about the bathers. We speculate about a couple
who go straight to the spa pool. It must be boiling,
you assume, noticing that no one stays
more than five minutes before easing back
into the lap pool. We watch a woman in her forties
with a son, about five. She stretches in the spa pool,

as if recovering from a sports injury, while
the little boy talks and talks. They make
faces at each other and it is then that I know
she's an actor – from an Australian sketch
show and a Taika Waititi film. I feel
more entitled to my voyeurism,
having watched her before, and less
entitled to this hotel room. What am I?
A teacher on unpaid maternity leave,
ordering room service and spying on
a celebrity playing with her child.
Tell us what it's like, my mother says,
apparently impressed at our choice
of accommodation, but tacitly disapproving
of the extravagance. We whine about not
being able to afford a house, yet buy
fourteen-dollar bags of coffee beans
and stay somewhere with valet parking.
It's for the baby, I imply – the late
check-out, the warmth and quiet –
everything now is for the baby.

13 December 2016

I try to lick off
what I think is a speck
of chocolate
I've dropped onto his fat
bare bicep but
find it permanent –
a mole or nevi. *When
do babies get moles?*
I googled last week as

we tried to keep his new skin
out of reach of the ozone
directly above my home
country. At four months,
it seems, exactly four months.
Watch it, my husband says,
and if it grows, changes texture
or is joined by a swarm of
other moles, we will go
to a paediatric dermatologist
to ensure it is not a tumour.
How could he, this boy
who the nurse says is thriving,
who is learning to kiss with a wide
open mouth and cannot stop
laughing when lying on his stomach
and listening to *A Lion in the Meadow*,
how could he have a tumour?
And I know this is only the first
sick question – what if and how
would I, and what would I do.

*

Peace at last,
the baby sleeps.
I write left-handed
so as not to disturb
but now he's awake,
full, but I offer him more
milk to prolong the peace
so that I may finish.[31]

31 To Finish

It is arbitrary; no real border any more. Thank goodness for minutes and days and months, and now years. Many senses of rest and end before death. The Latin *finire* means to set bounds or limits, from *finis* which suggests a division, a boundary. Initially, I said I would stop keeping this journal after the 'fourth trimester', or the three-month mark. But when November the 14th arrived, I wanted to keep writing. I still want to continue adding and adding, feeding and feeding (footnotes a sort of weaning), but without an end the tedium of all this eating and not sleeping and feeding and pacing would become diabolical, a circle of Dante's hell rather than his neon-lit heaven. And yet it does continue. (*You must go on. I can't go on. I'll go on.*) Our eyes adjust as the light changes.

This evening, after feeding from each breast, Robin crawled off my lap. Get *A Lion in the Meadow*, I suggested. He did, but instead of bringing it back to me, he slid off the bed on his tummy, backwards, as he has been taught to, holding on until his toes reach the floor, and then walked to the door and knocked on it, experimental. Do you want Dadda to read you your stories? I asked. He nodded. This has never happened before. You've been summoned, I told Nick, who had heard the conversation from the living room. Okay, let's read your stories, boy, and they closed the door behind me. Dinner was ready to grill, nothing to do but drink a glass of water and open the laptop for the fifteen minutes or so it would take for Robin to have his quota of reading.

The boundary between hurt and relief is unfenced and I wander between the two without knowing quite where I am. Finitude. An end; never a return to a previous state of being, but a conclusion to the last. This is the last story, I hear Nick say. Okay? Perhaps that is why I am struggling to wean, and always read about fifteen books and have the toddler scrabbling at my T-shirt as I try to put him into the cot. We all know I am less disciplined or respectful of edges. *Technically* is a word I use at school before ignoring a rule. But, the arbitrary – intellectual decisions, human-made and human-broken – is shaped by the necessary. The visceral truths of running out of milk, of a tender tendon behind your left knee when you run, of nearing middle age, of staring into the middle distance between the forking trunk of a eucalypt and seeing pale grey waves collapsing on wet sand and thinking helplessly of bereavement cards and the covers of Mills & Boon novels and admitting that the beach – nearly any beach; you're not that discerning – is your favourite place in the world. Your affinity with Ocean Beach is no surprise seeing as you were conceived there, Mum texted and I don't remember what, or if, I replied. Nonsense, the part of me shaped to fit alongside my husband thought; how could your place of conception affect your affinity with anything. (That would give Robin an innate affinity with petri dishes; to think we first saw him as a perfect new embryo, the strongest of the blastocysts!) But another part – possibly dating back to my personal 'big bang', when the cells started multiplying, or when, miraculous, my heart started beating by itself, this part loves to know and to have been told and to imagine. It is concrete knowledge I feel when the salt is drying tight on my skin and my ears are sore and eyes sting. Motherly candour – the unending sharing of bodies.

To Acknowledge

The people closest to *Neon Daze* haven't read it yet. Nick watched me writing, and distracted Robin when I needed time without toddler fingers jabbing at the keyboard. He knows that it's *personal* and records times of ugliness and utter strain. When I offered that he read the final draft and veto its submission to a publisher, he said no. He would wait for the published version. Thank you, Nick, for trusting me, for understanding my need to write, and for your love and care that is evident (but often underappreciated) in this book and every day.

Robin, you are still too young to wield your power of veto (regarding publication, at least), so I can only hope that eventually you'll understand why I wrote this during your first months. I hope you continue to like the cover ('That's your book cover!'), and to enjoy poems, and to know that I love you above all else. It is extraordinary good luck to be your mother.

Mum, I feel a similar luck to have you as my own mother despite being chronically poor at showing it. I remember you told me you thought I could be a writer, when I was about ten, and I haven't let go of that belief. Thank you for respecting me, loving me and teaching me to love and respect my own child.

Dad, when you play with Robin I remember you playing with me, and when I hear myself reading to Robin I hear your intonation. This was less obvious in the months the book records, but must have been there. It is a disorientating comfort, seeing us doubled in this way.

Paula, Patrick and Marion – the Australian side of Robin's whānau – thank you for becoming Grandma, Papa and The Aunt. Although you don't appear much in this book (I tried not to inflict that on you), you've been present and important, kind and understanding, during those months and since.

Thanks to Brigid, who – like family – has helped raise Robin and, unlike the original Mary Poppins, hasn't yet floated away holding an umbrella. We hope you never do.

Thanks to friends, who went there before us and handed down a bassinet, bottles, scraps of cloth, clothes, toys, blankets, a breast pump – stuff we didn't know we needed until we reached for it. Friends, who brought food, company, conversation, and love. Friends who are now Robin's friends too.

There were a few people who read or heard *Neon Daze* in its early stages and encouraged me to keep going. Anna Jackson, Angelina Sbroma and Helen Rickerby, thank you for organising Poetry and the Essay, a conference at Victoria University of Wellington in 2017, where I started to think that the scrawls in my notebooks could be called writing. I am especially grateful to Paula Green, Brian Blanchfield and Joan Fleming, who, one lunchtime, listened and counselled when I said I was afraid that since becoming a mother I didn't have the right to publish ever again. In particular, thanks to Brian for recommending Maggie Nelson's *The Argonauts*. Thanks to Joan for being the ideal first reader. And, thanks to Paula for sharing excerpts from *Neon Daze* on *NZ Poetry Shelf*.

Thanks, too, to Kent MacCarter at the *Cordite Poetry Review* for publishing a section.

Thanks to everyone at VUP: to Fergus for his honesty and open-mindedness, and to Kirsten and Craig for giving the book the best possible chance of being read. Thanks to Séraphine Pick and the Michael Lett Gallery for allowing us to use that exquisite drawing on the cover (once I saw the scribbly umbilical cord and placenta-like brain, I knew it was exactly right). And, so much gratitude to Ashleigh for editing with such sensitivity and tact.

It is a privilege to get any book published – to have the support to presume my voice is worth reading. *Neon Daze* records one unremarkable experience of the commonest phenomenon. Millions of women have been through those months without feeling the need or right (or having the time or health) to make a noise about it. Obviously I don't speak for any of them. But I'd like to acknowledge, as best I can, their grit. And the other millions of women who don't become mothers, for whatever reason – I want to acknowledge the value and validity of their experiences too. This book isn't meant as a veneration of maternity, just as a small, new view of something old and large, hopefully the kind of thing I was hungry for when I was pregnant.